A Feel Better Book

for Little Worriers

A FEEL BETTER BOOK
for Little Kids

For our mom, who's always there to make us feel better—HB & LB

*To all the little worriers out there—I hope that this book will provide
you with some useful tools to help keep the worries away*—SN-B

Text copyright © 2017 by Magination Press, an imprint of the
American Psychological Association. Illustrations copyright © 2017
by Shirley Ng-Benitez. All rights reserved. Except as permitted under
the United States Copyright Act of 1976, no part of this publication
may be reproduced or distributed in any form or by any means,
or stored in a database or retrieval system, without the prior written
permission of the publisher.

Published by
MAGINATION PRESS ®
An Educational Publishing Foundation Book
American Psychological Association
750 First Street NE
Washington, DC 20002

Magination Press is a registered trademark of the
American Psychological Association.

For more information about our books, including a complete catalog,
please write to us, call 1-800-374-2721, or visit our website at
www.apa.org/pubs/magination.

Book design by Susan K. White
Printed by Worzalla, Stevens Point, WI

Library of Congress Cataloging-in-Publication Data
Names: Brochmann, Holly, author. | Bowen, Leah, author. |
  Ng-Benitez, Shirley, illustrator.
Title: A feel better book for little worriers / by Holly Brochmann
and Leah Bowen ; Illustrated by Shirley Ng-Benitez.
Description: Washington, DC : Magination Press, American
Psychological Association, [2017] |
Summary: Illustrations and simple, rhyming text provide young
  children with tools for dealing with feelings of anxiety, such as
  breathing deeply or replacing worry with happy thoughts.
Identifiers: LCCN 2016040921| ISBN 9781433827181(hardcover)
 | ISBN 1433827182 (hardcover)
Subjects: | CYAC: Stories in rhyme. | Worry—Fiction.
Classification: LCC PZ8.3.B779 Fee 2017 | DDC [E]—dc23 LC record
available at https://lccn.loc.gov/2016040921

Manufactured in the United States of America
10 9 8 7 6 5 4 3 2 1

A Feel Better Book
for Little Worriers

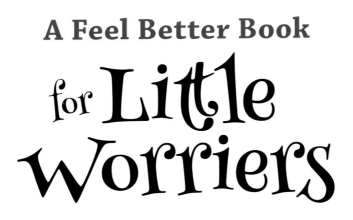

by Holly Brochmann and Leah Bowen
illustrated by Shirley Ng-Benitez

MAGINATION PRESS · WASHINGTON, DC
American Psychological Association

How's it going today,
are you doing all right?
Are you fantastic,
and happy and bright?

Or do you feel troubled
and perhaps a bit funny,
like butterflies are fluttering
around in your tummy?

Is your heart beating fast
like it's in a big hurry?
If your answer is yes,
then you might have a worry.

What is a worry?
It's thinking a thought
that something might happen
or that it might not.

The thoughts that you think
create feelings you feel.
They're no fun at all
and you wish they weren't real.

Worries are normal, they aren't always so bad. Everyone has them. Even Moms! Even Dads!

A worry can mean
different things, you see.

It might be one
thing for you,
and another for me.

So even though worries don't feel very good, and maybe you'd take them away if you could...

You should listen to them, those feelings inside. Are they helping or not? You'll have to decide.

Worries can be important,
they protect you from harm.
Sometimes there really is
a need for alarm!

Other times worries
are like a bad dream.
They can be pretty scary but
they aren't what they seem.

When these feelings take over
and bring your whole day down,
there are things you can do
to help turn it around.

Let's practice together
just you and me.
First take a deep breath,
then two, then three!

Jump up and down,
spin 'til you're dizzy!
Your brain feels better
when your body is busy.

Then stand up tall.
Stretch your arms up high.
Take another big breath
and reach for the sky!

Now let your breath out
steady and slow,
and dangle your arms
to the floor down below.

One last breath in through your nose,
through your mouth let it out.
Imagine your body
feels heavy throughout.

Close your eyes
and pretend
just like when
you play.
Put that worry
in a box
and throw it
away!

Throw it deep
in the ocean,

worry

bury it in the sand
on the beach.

Cast it up
in a tree
too far out
of reach.

Your worry is fading
so with no more delays,
let's lead your thoughts
to a happier place!

What makes you laugh?
What makes you smile?
Is it sweet treats you eat
every once in a while?

Or is it a toy that's better
than all of the rest?
Think of your favorite,
the one you like best.

So when worries get stuck
inside of your head,
try switching your thoughts
to happy ones instead!

But perhaps the most important
thing you should do,
is tell someone you trust
because they can help too.

So don't keep those feelings
tucked deep down inside.
You're braver than you think,
you'll be so glad you tried!

And if that worry comes back
some other time,
you will know what to do,
just remember this rhyme!

Note to Parents & Caregivers

Imagine if the skills for managing stress and anxiety were learned at a young age—children who are experiencing anxious feelings for the first time would be able to practice proper breathing and relaxation techniques to help ease their worries. Teaching these skills early in a child's life will not only establish confidence and courage, but will set the foundation for managing anxiety that can transition well into adulthood.

How This Book Can Help

A *Feel Better Book for Little Worriers* offers an interactive approach that not only teaches little worriers to recognize anxiety as it's happening, but provides them with simple coping mechanisms they will look forward to practicing day after day. Each verse offers a valuable lesson. Whether using this book at home, school, or in a clinical setting, these lessons can be put to use in a multitude of ways.

Learning About Anxiety

Learning to recognize anxiety, while it may seem obvious to adults, can be a big step for a child. Here are some key things to pay attention to when introducing this concept to a child:

- **Body awareness**
  Is your heart beating fast, like it's in a big hurry? An anxious feeling, often described as a "pit in our stomach" or "nervous butterflies," generally originates as a thought in our mind. As we learn how our bodies and minds are connected, we can then begin to understand why we are feeling a particular sensation. Do we have those butterflies because we are about to try something new? Or perhaps our heart is racing because we sense danger is near. Recognizing and identifying these feelings in our bodies is a key ingredient to understanding anxiety, and while a young child probably will not comprehend all the complexities of this principle, they can certainly begin to

understand the concept of the mind and body connection.

- **Defining anxiety**
  What is a worry? Worries and fears develop quite early in a child's life, well before they are even aware of the existence of anxiety. This book offers a simple definition, in child friendly terms, that will help children identify what a worry is and when one arrives. Armed with this knowledge, children no longer have to keep their worries trapped inside and instead are able to communicate when they are feeling anxious, enabling them to seek help from their caregivers in finding ways to "feel better."
- **Normalizing**
  Even moms! Even dads! Letting a child know they are not alone in their worries will help them feel more comfortable when experiencing anxiety. For instance, your child tells you he is worried about going to the dentist. A parent could respond, "I understand that. Lots of people are scared of going to the dentist, even grownups. Let's talk about what will happen so you'll know what to expect, and then we can practice some of your breathing exercises before you go."

Recognizing and Distinguishing Between Worries

Sometimes we get so caught up in our feelings that it's difficult to recognize what specifically is causing them. Learning to slow down and pay attention to our bodies and our feelings can help us manage them.

- **Listening to your body**
  You should listen to them, those feelings inside. Once a child is able to identify their feelings as worries, they must then learn to interpret what the worries mean. Learning to listen to the cues your body is sending you is a skill that can help with worry identification, boundary setting, and self-control.

- **Some worries are good**
  They protect you from harm. It is important for children to know that some anxiety is not only normal, but can actually be very important and useful. While not having any anxiety would be quite peaceful, it would also stop our body from naturally telling us that we are putting ourselves in a potentially dangerous situation. For example, anxiety should be present around strangers or when crossing a busy street.
- **But…some worries *aren't* useful**
  They aren't what they seem. When levels of anxiety consistently interfere with day-to-day activities and routines, there are things you can do. First, caregivers must recognize that a child's anxiety has surpassed a "healthy" limit. Children are often not emotionally mature enough to explain what they are feeling, so when their anxiety reaches this level they will sometimes demonstrate these feelings in other ways. Is she afraid in situations most children find exciting and fun? Does she seem withdrawn or depressed? Is she cautious more than she is carefree? Encouraging children to talk about their feelings, especially physical ones, can help bring hidden worries to the surface.

Tools for Managing Anxiety

And of course, once we have learned to recognize feelings, we want to manage them! The following are some helpful tools for dealing with anxiety and worries.

- **Just breathe**
  Take a deep breath, then two, then three! Anxiety causes physical changes to take place in the body that actually make symptoms feel worse. Teaching children to stretch their limbs and to take long, deep breaths allows them to take in more oxygen and to slow their heartbeat. One method for helping young children learn to take deep breaths is to pretend they are smelling a candle (in through your nose), then blowing it gently out (out through your mouth). You can also teach children to take deep belly breaths by asking them to lay down and place a small item, such as a toy, on their belly. They can watch the toy move slowly up and down as their breath moves in and out.
- **Get moving**
  Spin 'til you're dizzy! Numerous studies have shown the positive effects of exercise on anxiety. Like breathing, movement increases the flow of oxygen in the body and also releases endorphins, both of which automatically deescalate the physical symptoms of anxiety.
- **Visualize**
  Imagine putting that worry in a box and throwing it away! Visualization is a technique often used to help adults with anxiety, and it works just as well for children. The example the book suggests is to visualize a worry box, but caregivers can take this suggestion even further and work with the child to actually create a worry box, bringing the visualizations to life. The child can write about a worry or draw what it looks like, place it in a special box you create together (such as a decorated shoebox), and "throw" the worry away by setting the box out of reach and out of sight. This activity empowers children by allowing them to exercise physical control over their worries while channeling their feelings through a specific action. Repeat as often as necessary, allowing the child to come back to the worry for additional processing, adding more worries to the box, or ripping up old worries that are no longer present.
- **Positive thinking**
  What makes you smile? After a worry has been addressed and processed, happy thoughts can help children feel more at ease. In fact, the more happy thoughts you think, the better you feel overall. Suggest recalling a happy memory, such as opening gifts on Christmas morning, or a happy place, such as Grandpa's farm. But perhaps the most effective way to help a child have a positive outlook on life is to model one.

- **You aren't alone**
  Tell someone you trust. It is important for children to learn they are not alone. You can also help children articulate their feelings—which is often difficult for them to do—by prompting them with questions, such as "Do you feel flutters in your tummy?" or "Do you feel calm or do you feel scared?" If their answer suggests they may be experiencing anxiety, assure them that the two of you will get through it together. Ultimately, the goal is for them to learn the physical and emotional "symptoms" of anxiety and have the confidence to come to you when they are worried.
- **Encouragement**
  You're braver than you think. Offer encouragement and commend the child for facing challenges head on. Young worriers will not only be more comfortable seeking your guidance with future anxious episodes, but will build both courage and confidence—valuable attributes that will serve them throughout life in a multitude of ways.

A Final Thought

Anxiety is experienced by every child on some level, so the exercises in this book can be useful for addressing both excessive worries and the smaller worries that are a part of everyday life. While this book is aimed at giving caregivers simple and effective tools to use at home, in school, or as a clinical supplement, a parent or caregiver should seek additional professional help if they feel it is necessary. Please contact your child's pediatrician or school counselor for licensed mental health professional referrals.

About the Authors

Sisters LEAH BOWEN and HOLLY BROCHMANN are dedicated wives, mothers, and authors, each passionate about contributing to a mentally healthier society in a meaningful way. Leah has a Master of Education degree in counseling with a focus in play therapy. She is a Licensed Professional Counselor and Registered Play Therapist in the state of Texas where she currently practices, and she is committed to helping her child clients work through issues including abuse, depression, and anxiety. Holly can trace her earliest memories of anxiety back to the young age of four, and she is an advocate for managing common mental health issues through therapy and exercise. She has a degree in journalism and enjoys creative writing both as a hobby and as a primary part of her career in public relations.

About the Illustrator

SHIRLEY NG-BENITEZ loves to draw! Fond memories of her youth, nature, and her two daughters inspire her mixed media illustrations. Since '98, she's owned gabbyandco.com, her design, illustration, and lettering firm, and is now living her dream illustrating and writing picture books in San Martin, CA, with her husband, daughters, and pup. Shirley's very honored to have illustrated this book, her third published by Magination Press. You can find more of her work on her website, www.shirleyngbenitez.com.

About Magination Press

MAGINATION PRESS is an imprint of the American Psychological Association, the largest scientific and professional organization representing psychologists in the United States and the largest association of psychologists worldwide.

Hollywood

The Pioneers

front end paper] Buster Keaton,
as a small-town projectionist
in *Sherlock, Jr* (1924).

PLEASE
BE SILENT
BEHIND CAMERA

VON STERNBERG

MPGP-49

HOLLYWOOD
The Pioneers

by KEVIN BROWNLOW

Photographs Selected by

JOHN KOBAL

ALFRED A. KNOPF   NEW YORK, 1979

THIS IS A BORZOI BOOK
PUBLISHED BY ALFRED A. KNOPF, INC.

Copyright © 1979 Thames Television, Kevin Brownlow

All rights reserved under International and Pan-American Copyright Conventions.

Published in the United States by Alfred A. Knopf, Inc., New York.
Distributed by Random House, Inc., New York.
Originally published in England by William Collins Sons & Co. Ltd., London.

Library of Congress Cataloging in Publication Data

Brownlow, Kevin.
Hollywood—the pioneers.

1. Silent films—History and criticism.
2. Moving-Pictures—United States—History.
I. Title.
PN1995.75.B7   1979   791.43'0973   79-2297
ISBN 0-394-50851-3

Manufactured in the United States of America
First American Edition

frontispiece] It was known as the silent era, but there was nothing silent about it. Films were shown with musical accompaniment— in the big theatres this often meant a combination of symphony orchestra and theatre organ. And on the set, the noise of carpenters hammering sets, other companies making other films, could be deafening—which was why director Josef von Sternberg insisted on this sign. Conrad Nagel (left), Matthew Betz (behind sign) and Renée Adorée pose for a gag shot behind cameraman Maximilian Fabian and von Sternberg during the shooting of MGM's *Escape*, later titled *Exquisite Sinner* (1926).

Contents

Acknowledgements

If one aim of the television series is to capture for posterity the first-hand recollections of the veterans of the silent era, the aim of this book is to make available some of the most evocative still pictures of the period. Very few of them have been published before. Several collectors, including Marc Wanamaker, of Bison Art, Los Angeles (whose own book on the studios will be a reference work of great importance), Bruce Torrence, John E. Allen, Bob Birchard, and such agencies as Culver Pictures, Brown Brothers, the National Film Archive and the Museum of Modern Art, have supplied rare photographs. Some are from my own files, but the majority come from the archive of John Kobal, who has built up his remarkable collection over the past decade with uncanny skill. Thanks to him, we have been able to work, in most cases, direct from the original, retaining as much as possible of the pictorial quality.

This book is essentially a collection of photographs, and my text serves as a set of rails to provide a smooth ride for those unfamiliar with the territory. The route is well worn—Edison, Porter, Griffith—essential signposts in any journey through the complex byways of film history. I have also included extracts from as many as possible of the interviews we obtained for the series.

For further reading, William K. Everson has published an excellent and concise survey, *American Silent Film*. George Pratt's *Spellbound in Darkness* is an invaluable source book. Karl Brown has written what must rank as the most enjoyable, and the most vivid, volume of motion-picture memoirs in *Adventures with D. W. Griffith*. Of my own books, *The Parade's Gone By . . .* examines the American silent film through interviews with those who created it; and *The War, the West and the Wilderness* is a treasure hunt through archives and film collections in search of history on film—the history of World War One, the old West and the great expeditions.

Other books which helped me compile this one include Lewis Jacobs's *Rise of the American Film*; Gordon Hendricks's *The Edison Motion Picture Myth*; *The American Film Industry*, edited by Tino Balio; *The Movies* by Richard Griffith and Arthur Mayer; *Hollywood, the Golden Age* by Jack Spears; *The History of the American Film Industry* by Benjamin Hampton; *The American Film Institute Catalogue of Feature Films* 1921–30, (what a tragedy the AFI decided not to fund their catalogue of 1916–20 to completion); Alexander Walker's *Stardom* and *Valentino*; David Robinson's *Hollywood in the 'Twenties*; John Baxter's *Hollywood Exiles*; Thomas Cripp's *Slow Fade to Black*; *Histoire Générale du Cinema*, which Bernard Eisenschitz compiled from material left by the late Georges Sadoul; and such source material as *Moving Picture World*, *Photoplay*, *Picture Play*, *Motion Picture Magazine*.

Grateful thanks to all those who worked on the series, whose names are contained in the credits, especially to David Gill, Sue McConachy and Barry O'Riordan. My gratitude, too, to Vivien Bowler, William K. Everson, George Pratt, John Edwards, Pat Montgomery, Richard Schickel, David Bradley, Alexander Walker, R. Davies, Roger Reed, Frank Holland, Jim Wilde, Raymond Fielding, Mary Corliss, Richard Koszarski, Russell Merritt, Pru Reading, Simon Crocker, Michael Sissons, Philip Ziegler, Ronald Clark, Trevor Vincent, Shirley McAuley and Julie Richardson, Karl Malkames—and special thanks to my wife, Virginia, whose reaction I relied upon when selecting the pictures.

Preface

Talk to people who saw films for the first time when they were silent, and they will tell you the experience was magic. The silent film, with music, had extraordinary powers to draw an audience into the story, and an equally potent capacity to make their imagination work. They had to supply the voices and the sound effects, and because their minds were engaged, they appreciated the experience all the more. The audience was the final creative contributor to the process of making a film.

The films have gained a charm and other-worldliness with age but, inevitably, they have also lost something. The impression they made when there was no rival to the moving picture was more profound, more intense; compared to the easily accessible pictures of today, it was the blow of a two-handed axe, against the blunt scraping of a tableknife.

The films belong to an era considered simpler and more desirable than our own. But nostalgia should not be allowed to cast a Portobello Road quaintness over the past, for it obliges us to edit from our mind the worst aspects of a period and embrace only those elements we admire. The silent period may be known as 'The Age of Innocence' but it included years unrivalled for their dedicated viciousness. In Europe, between 1914 and 1918 more men were killed to less purpose than at any other time in history. In America, men who stood out from the herd—pacifists, anarchists, socialists —were rounded up and deported in 1919, and were lucky to avoid being lynched. The miseries of war culminated in the miseries of disease when the Spanish flu swept Europe and America and killed more civilians than the war had killed soldiers. With peace came the Versailles treaty—collapse and starvation in Central Europe—the idealism of Prohibition—gangsterism in America.

The benefit of the moving picture to a care-worn populace was inestimable, but the sentimentality and charm, the easily understandable, black-and-white issues were not so much a reflection of everyday life as a means of escape from it. Again and again, in the publications of the time, one reads horrified reactions against films showing 'life as it is'.

You did not leave the problems of home merely to encounter them again at the movies. You paid your money, initially, for forgetfulness. As the company slogans put it: 'Mutual Movies Make Time Fly' . . . 'Selznick Pictures Create Happy Hours'. And if the experience took you out of yourself and excited you, you talked about it to your friends and fellow-workers, creating the precious 'word of mouth' publicity that the industry depended upon. You may have exaggerated a little, but the movies soon matched your hyperbole. They evolved to meet the demands of their audience.

Gradually movie-going altered from relaxation to ritual. In the big cities, you went to massive picture palaces, floating through incense-laden air to the strains of organ music, to worship at the Cathedral of Light. You paid homage to your favourite star; you dutifully communed with the fan magazines. You wore the clothes they wore in the movies; you bought the furniture you saw on the screen. You joined a congregation composed of every strata of society. And you shared your adulation with Shanghai, Sydney and Santiago. For your favourite pastime had become the most powerful cultural influence in the world—exceeding even that of the Press. The silent film was not only a vigorous popular art; it was a universal language—Esperanto for the eyes.

Regret for the passing of the silent film is no longer regarded as a symptom of advancing age; the art form has acquired a legion of admirers in the last few years. A surprising number of films, written off as lost, have been rediscovered, and their message is that the silent era was far more inventive than anyone had thought. The great names— D. W. Griffith, King Vidor and F. W. Murnau—retain their crowns, but a second echelon of brilliant film-makers has been revealed. John Collins was a young director of enormous talent who, had he not died in the 1918 flu epidemic, would certainly have been one of the giants of film history. Reginald Barker, it turns out, made many of the best films attributed to Thomas Ince—*Wrath of the Gods, The Coward* and *The Italian*. In terms of cinematic action, Allen Holubar was probably better than Griffith, as was Francis Ford, if only in his films for the Ince company. And a woman director, Lois Weber, made pictures which were exceptionally strong, both in their emotional and in their technical values.

The system that produced the films was, then as now, aimed at profit. To characterise the men concerned with the financial side as visionaries, the lamp of truth gleaming in their eyes, would be ridiculous. Some of them remained the racketeers they had been before taking up the picture business.

The men and women who did the creative work were a different breed. They, too, were motivated by money. Many took the job simply because it paid so well. But I have yet to meet a director or cameraman who did not love his job, and who was not enthralled by the magic at his fingertips. I have acquired a deep affection for these pioneers; they had a spirit and an *élan* that is highly appealing in our own day when the film industry is ruled by giant conglomerates. Theirs was a much more leisurely time, and yet they worked fast. The silent feature arrived and departed within fifteen years. And by 1927 Hollywood was turning out an average of 700 silent features a year.

If there is one word that sums up the attitude of the silent film-makers, that word is enthusiasm. It is conveyed most strongly in the films of the 'teens, before the formulas had taken shape—when there was more room for experiment.

"They didn't know what they were working in," said Agnes de Mille. "They didn't know what the future would be. They knew that every picture broke boundaries. Some one new thing would be done, a new way of handling the camera, a new way of cutting, a new way of lighting, and they'd be so excited by it. My father used to say 'We are not real artists. We are like the pre-Elizabethan dramatists. They were not really great poets, but they made it possible for the next generation, and the generation after, to become great artists and great poets.' "

The style of the 'teens was exuberant but tentative, in marked contrast to the stolid style of earlier years, when films were often photographed stage plays. Their enthusiastic uncertainty often resulted in surprises— accidentally discovered techniques, such as pyrotechnic editing or startling travelling shots. Some films display experiments with players, like the 1915 gangster film, *Regeneration*, shot in the Lower East Side of New York with real gangsters, bums and streetwalkers providing local colour of the most startling kind. Other films, particularly those of Thomas Ince, provided tragic endings as often as other companies supplied happy ones. (These, too, disappeared, as the industry grew to know its public.)

By the 1920s, the Americans knew exactly how to make pictures, and they made them with great proficiency. The surprises offered by the formative years were replaced by richer, more mature films, the best of which were outstanding works of art. The 1920s were the golden decade of film-making. And not just in America; this was the period when such men as Eisenstein in Russia, Abel Gance in France, Fritz Lang in Germany, were creating a new prestige for the cinema.

The finest films of the twenties were distinguished by highly intelligent writing and direction, brilliant acting and superb camerawork. Yet they depended on two further elements which we can seldom provide today—a large and receptive audience, and a well-orchestrated score. For the audience, the fusion of picture and music added up to far more than the sum of the respective parts. The effect was that of two carbons in an arc-lamp which, when brought together, create a light of unbelievable intensity.

The popular art of today, television, is not an ideal medium for the presentation of silent films; the audience is separate, and the electronic system is incompatible with the subtlety of silent-era photography. Carefully studied

diffusion simply looks soft. To overcome these problems for the series, Thames Television has spent enormous sums to acquire the best prints, and to ensure the correct speed. Silent films were photographed at different speeds to sound films—speeds which could vary wildly. Thames has used a special machine called a Polygon to slow the film down, and by transferring direct to videotape, as much quality as possible has been preserved. Many of the old films will look very good on television, but the electronic version can never be compared to the projected image.

Condemned as we are to view the cinema of the past through a glass darkly, what hope have future generations of seeing the films as they were meant to be seen? Very little. The stock on which the films were photographed—nitrate— is highly dangerous, and is now virtually outlawed. It can be copied, of course, but black-and-white stock is gradually being phased out, and has lost much of its old quality. This is partly due to the fact that the laboratory veterans, who knew how to handle it, have retired, and the young men, skilled with colour, are mere beginners by comparison.

As a result, the vast majority of silent films survive today in prints which make nonsense of the work the original technicians put into them. The fact that so few people care— least of all laboratories and distribution libraries—ensures that the practice will persist.

They took immense care with the photographic quality in the silent days because it was all they had. A silent film depended on its visuals; as soon as you degrade those, you lose elements that go far beyond the image on the surface. You remove the possibility of enjoyment.

A film which seems dull in a poor dupe (the industry term for duplicate) can leap to life in a first-class print. Suddenly you realise you can see the faces—and facial expressions were very important. The acting in silents was often very subtle, very restrained, despite legends to the contrary. Being unable to see the facial expressions in a silent film is like trying to enjoy a horse-race without seeing the horses.

The drama was inextricably entwined with the quality of photography, not just for the reason that you could see better, but from the point of view of mood. *The Cat and the Canary* (1927), a send-up of Gothic ghost stories, had some marvellously spooky lighting effects which registered as an annoying, muddy flicker on the first print I saw. I therefore ignored the film until, years later, I saw a crisp and beautiful print from a foreign archive. The difference was extraordinary. I now regard *The Cat and the Canary* as one of the best pictures of the twenties. Yet, typically, the good print remains buried in an archive; the version available to the public is a barely-visible 16 mm dupe.

Jerky and flickery the modern versions of silent films may be, but the vast picture palaces didn't attract four to six thousand people a night by giving them eyestrain.

"Print quality is enormously important in the appreciation of a film," said James Card, retired curator of George Eastman House. "This is something that we archivists and film teachers have failed to recognise and appreciate. It's one thing for us to see *Intolerance* in a battered, murky, sixth generation print, because we've seen it before in finer prints somewhere along the line. But for people to see it for the first time in such atrocious form is to delude them and to deprive them of any recognition of what a fine, beautifully photographed, delicately mounted, original release print should look like.

"There are so few of the basic classics around that even have a vague resemblance to the original. Fairbanks's *Thief of Bagdad* is an example; in a poor print, this film is nothing. But seeing one of those original release prints, with the blending of the tinting and the dawn effects, where the colour comes slowly into the clouds and slowly fades out again—it's just an extraordinary experience. No black and white duplicate, however beautifully graded, can equal it. Anything less than that is just not that film—it's some other film. You can't take a painting of Titian's, for example, as a cheap colour reproduction in a book, and have the slightest conception of what the painting is like in reality."

Aesthetics apart, what is the justification for preserving the silent film? Do the films have some intrinsic value? I think they do. Part of the importance of any film lies in the period in which it was made. This applies particularly to the silent film, for it represents the earliest part of our history covered by moving pictures. Directly or indirectly, the kaleidoscope of dreams, aspirations, prejudices, loves and loathings of a dead epoch comes to life again with undiminished authenticity on the screen. A precious factor of a film, say, 1921, was that it was made in 1921. It is not a period confection like *The Sting*, which depends on instantly recognisable signals and symbols to induce nostalgia. You may see a still from a film of 1921 and recognise nothing about it. The clothes may seem exaggerated, the make-up overdone, the urban landscape that of another planet. But once the picture itself gets under way, you will experience a distillation of another time.

This is beyond value, whether you care about film technique or not. The movies are the nearest we will ever get to H. G. Wells's *Time Machine*. History as a subject demands massive research before one can acquire the empathy that a film, through entertainment, can provide instantaneously.

*　　*　　*

"You won't find anyone left but me," said Gloria Swanson, when we asked her for an interview, and this might seem a reasonable reflection, given that the silent era ended half a century ago. But we found, to our relief, that a surprisingly large number of veterans had survived, with their memories —and much of their energy—intact.

Generalisations about people—particularly such individualistic people as the movie crowd—can only provide the most superficial hints of their personalities.

But one thing that strikes you at once is their humour. Behind it, you can sense the enjoyment that must have been such an integral part of early film making.

We made allowances for the fact that almost all the people we talked to were old. Adults in the twenties must now be well over seventy; some of those we talked to were in their nineties. Yet none of them were 'elderly' in the sense of being feeble or slow-witted. Quite the opposite. They had retained their quickness of mind, their charm and their fascination with the art of making pictures.

Not that everyone was willing to be interviewed. Some, like Pola Negri, were horrified at the idea, clutching at a ragbag of excuses but finally admitting that they were terrified of what the camera might show after fifty years. To cope with this problem, we took Bessie Love with us on our second trip to the United States. A silent star from 1915, Bessie Love had left Hollywood for England in 1935, and hadn't been back for thirty years. We knew she could open doors that would have remained closed to us.

Mary Astor, for instance, was in hospital at the Motion Picture Home. Mary Astor is Bessie Love's sister-in-law. She, too, began in silents, and starred opposite John Barrymore in such films as *Don Juan* (1926). Bessie Love visited her in hospital, and tentatively broached the idea of an interview. Absolutely no, said Mary Astor; she was far too ill, there was no chance. But Bessie Love has little respect for illness, and I was a witness to the magical transformation she effected in Mary Astor's condition.

Much against her better judgement, Mary Astor found herself facing the camera. She was still beautiful, and very funny, with a healthy 'Oh, baloney!' attitude to the myths of the past. As the camera rolled, she became more and more animated. By the end, she had to admit she had enjoyed herself. The following day, well ahead of schedule, she was discharged from hospital and sent home.

I had already carried out a number of interviews on tape during my first visit to Hollywood in 1964, which resulted in my book, *The Parade's Gone By* . . . Now I had the opportunity of capturing the interviews on film. Susan McConachy moved ahead of the camera team, talking to the people I didn't know. She recorded several unique interviews on tape, including the last conducted with Bryan Foy, the director of the first all-talking feature *The Lights of New York*; he died suddenly, just as we reached America.

The films about Hollywood depict a narrow group of types: the brutal producer, the cynical writer, the alcoholic star and the flotsam and jetsam surrounding them. Like all stereotypes, such people existed. But in my experience, the film makers of the pioneering days were a much more colourful breed. Hollywood films have never done justice, for instance, to their expressive turn of phrase, which linked them so strongly to their period. I remember asking a cameraman a simple question about the heat of the lights at a particular studio. I might have elicited a dull answer; "Yes, they were hot." But this cameraman knew how to convey an idea. "Hot?" he said. "You could light a cigar on the beam at a hundred yards."

Compared to their counterparts today, the early film people might seem innocent. It's not entirely true, of course, but they had an attractive, almost ingenuous optimism. They were often tough, funny, kind, sentimental, and most that I have met were immensely likeable.

I thought I was prejudiced in my affection for these people—seldom can a historian have had so pleasant an assignment as to go from one to the other, recording their memories. But I was delighted to find my enthusiasm reflected in the faces and remarks of the crew, as they emerged from each interview: "*What* an amazing person!"

No doubt the Hollywood people had the full range of what would now be called neuroses—for many of them were given a rough passage in the cause of entertainment. But, in the silent era, the industry was not the high-pressured assembly-line business it became later—a business that consumed people like industrial fuel. While some of the veterans were safely out of it by then, others went through the whole epoch from galloping tintypes to television. It was these people who usually held the warmest memories for the early days—for they had experienced the full shock of all the changes.

Of course they concentrated upon the incidents. Few of them were articulate about aesthetics. The making of films was a job which they enjoyed, but which they went about in an intuitive way. Trying to get them to analyse their technique was a futile operation and one certain to lead to a rapid change of subject.

Precise historical accuracy is not what one expects from these interviews. No one has instant recall for the order of events, nor for the exact date on which they occurred. What they can provide is the life that gives such dates meaning—the spirit of the time. I was surprised how well most people remembered the events of fifty, sixty years ago. Director Allan Dwan described vividly his arrival in California, in search of a lost movie company, in 1911. Viola Dana recalled her sister's dialogue in an Edison talking picture of 1913; by chance we found the film, with its sound—and the dialogue matched. Some of the memories turn myths inside out—that Rudolph Valentino was an untalented lounge-lizard or that John Gilbert lost his job because his voice was squeaky.

We were unable to use all the interviews but, fortunately, Thames Television made a large donation to the National Film Archive to enable it to preserve them all.

Pioneers are people of exceptional energy—a quality that sets them apart. An example of this occurred at the Sun Valley Western Conference in 1976, which David Gill and I attended. We encountered the director, Henry King, who had once been a pilot. He was known as the Flying Director. I asked him if he still flew from time to time. "I flew in this morning," he said. "Oh, I realise that," I said, thinking of the twin-engined boneshaker which had transported us all across the mountains. "But do you ever fly your own plane?"

"I flew in my own plane this morning," he replied. We could only blink in astonished admiration—for King's career goes back almost as far as powered flight.

"I'm a pioneer," said fellow-director King Vidor, when I told him this story, "I've been in this business for years. But even when I first got to Hollywood, Henry King was going strong."

It is impossible to listen to these people without marvelling; they are so extraordinary in their old age . . . what must Hollywood have been like when they were all young? This book tries to find out.

Kevin Brownlow

Preface by John Kobal

The Men Who Shot the Stills

In 1901 a photograph was taken of a film being shot in Edison's little New York studio. It was for an article in a German newspaper about that new American invention 'the movies', and it was probably the first still—a picture of a scene being shot taken with a plate camera mounted on a tripod rather than merely an enlargement of a frame from a film—to be used for the purpose of promoting a film in the media. Three-quarters of a century have gone by since then, millions of stills have been taken and distributed to whet our appetites for thousands of films, and they nearly all have one thing in common with that first still—we don't know who took them. Mac Julian, Fred Archer, Sherman Clark, Ray Jones, Madison Lacy, Frank Powolny, Milton Browne, Jimmy Manatt, John Miehle, Bud Longworth, William Grimes, Kenneth Alexander . . . these are a few of the names which we look for in vain in the mass of movie books, almost everyone of which uses, but never acknowledges, the work of these men—the early still photographers.

The lack of regard accorded to still photographers

outside the industry was a result of their treatment within it. It was extremely rare for them to work with a director like DeMille, Frank Borzage or Josef von Sternberg who did not merely tolerate but actually aided the still photographer at his job. In the main, the nature of their work, though providing vital publicity, was treated by the creators as peripheral to the making of the movie and the still men were seen as a nuisance to be tolerated. A typical reaction from directors and crews was "Hurry the darn thing!"

By 1918 the taking of stills, previously done by cameramen or assistants on the set, had become a function in its own right, and the still men, whatever their responsibility to the publicity departments who needed their work, were not confidence men faking facts but pioneer photo-journalists recording history in the making. As such they took the same risks and hardships that were part and parcel of the cameraman's lot on location. But while the big productions could have as many as ten cameras set up to capture the action, there would be only one still photographer to record it all. As hundreds of wagons raced across the plains in *Tumbleweeds* (1925), as the cattle stampeded in *The Iron Horse* (1924), as the Israelites fled from the Egyptians in *The Ten Commandments* (1923), and the prospectors trekked up the icy slopes in *Trail of '98* (1928), the still man was right there to the left of the cameraman, vividly capturing the immediacy of the action to ensure that the public's expectations for the films would be well and truly aroused.

In many cases the still photographers' work is our only record of films which have been lost through fire, flood, theft or simple wear and tear, and of others whose prints are so rare that they must remain locked away in archives until the money becomes available for copies to be made. For decades, before the fashion for revivals which characterised the sixties, people who had never seen a Griffith film sensed something of his genius through the still taken of the staggering Babylonian set for *Intolerance* (1916). The torrid Gilbert/Garbo romance, which symbolised the roaring twenties, came alive through a still from *Love* (1927)—one of the most widely reproduced pictures in the history of photography.

I can still recall what an eye-opener the Richard Griffith/Arthur Mayer book, *The Movies*, was for me when it first appeared. Marvellous reproductions of original prints ensured that the pioneer works of the cinema sprang to life. Seeing them, movie history—about which

I knew nothing—took on an energy and dynamism to equal that of the contemporary films in which I was immersed. Through stills like these, the world of the silent movies was opened up to me as vibrant and immediate as it must have been on the day the films were made. The stills drew my attention to the extraordinary visual quality of silent films and to lighting techniques which created effects as rich and subtle as those of the great painters and possessed an almost three-dimensional depth.

But who took these photos? Until the formation of their union in 1928 and the start of their house magazine, *The International Photographer*, which occasionally discussed their work, virtually no records exist to tell us which photographers worked on which films—I have combined the memories of the surviving photographers from the period with some guesswork of my own, based largely on available information about which photographers were under contract to which studio. However, many of the large studios, like Paramount, were releasing some seventy films a year and employing only four or five still men, anyone of whom might have worked on two or three productions at a time. Unlike their brothers working in the portrait galleries, the still photographer did not have his own lighting set-up but had to use the lighting for the film camera. So we do not even have individual lighting styles to guide in guessing who photographed the stills on which film. What we do have, despite the extraordinary odds against which these photographers worked—with heavy cameras and slow film—is a body of work that is witness to the technical excellence and the sheer exuberance all the Hollywood still men brought to their work as individuals, and this contribution no lighting man could give them or take away.

For every still which I am able to credit to a photographer, thousands remain to be researched. Occasionally I might come across an old fan magazine which has reproduced a still with a credit, but my best source of information is an original print from the period, for they sometimes have the photographer's name on the back. I share the burden of this research with all those who write about the movies. We all owe a debt to the still photographers, for, as once they helped sell the movies, so now they help sell the books about the movies. This book is a tribute to them.

John Kobal

133-68

15

Monte Blue in *White Shadows of the South Seas* (1928)
directed by W. S. Van Dyke;
cameraman, Clyde de Vinna.

Lon Chaney (centre) and Shirley Mason in *Treasure Island* (1920)
directed by Maurice Tourneur;
cameraman, René Guissart.

right] John Barrymore as *Don Juan* (1926)
directed by Alan Crosland;
cameraman, Byron Haskin.

Ralph Forbes and Harry Carey in *Trail of '98* (1928)
directed by Clarence Brown;
cameraman John Seitz.

Alice Terry in *Mare Nostrum* (1926)
directed by Rex Ingram;
cameraman, John Seitz.

4244

22

Louise Dresser in *The Goose Woman* (1925)
directed by Clarence Brown;
cameraman, Milton Moore.

George Bancroft in *Docks of New York* (1928)
directed by Josef von Sternberg;
cameraman, Hal Rosson.

CHAPTER TWO

Suspension of Disbelief

Edison and Invention

A T the end of the nineteenth century, the public, in Europe and America, had grown accustomed to the astonishing rate at which new discoveries were brightening their lives. They termed it 'white magic'. They couldn't understand the inventions, any more than we can understand how to send men to the moon, but they were confident that they were living in the greatest age in history, and that inventors were the flowers of that age.

A number of men, in Europe and America, were struggling to make pictures move. Photography had made immense progress in its first half-century, yet a forest of obstacles stood in the way of anyone who tried to bring photographs to life. Fortunately, ideas seemed to generate like wireless waves across the globe, and if one inventor found his way around one obstacle, his success propelled the experiments of a dozen others.

In America, where history is ascribed to individuals rather than to groups, the name of Thomas Alva Edison had come to represent all that was great in the field of inventions. Having produced the electric light bulb and the phonograph, he was naturally expected to produce the moving picture. Yet he displayed little interest in its development, regarding it as a toy and reserving his creative enthusiasm for the phonograph.

The rapid progress of European inventors, however, imperilled his reputation, and so Edison's imagination supplied the moving picture long before his workshop produced it. Still obsessed with sound, he announced, in 1891:

"I hope to be able by the invention to throw upon a canvas a perfect picture of anybody, and reproduce his words. Thus, should Patti be singing somewhere, this invention will put her full length picture upon the canvas so perfectly as to enable one to distinguish every feature and expression of her face, see all her actions and listen to the entrancing melody of her peerless voice. I have already perfected the invention so far as to be able to picture a prize fight— the two men, the ring, the intensely interested faces of those surrounding it—and you can hear the sound of the blows."

False claims, self-aggrandisement and hyperbole are the stuff of motion picture history, but this description must take a special place in the annals of mendacity. For it describes not only moving pictures, but live television—and it led to a flurry of supposition and inaccuracy in the world's press. Edison seemed to have invented everything else, so convenience laid this new achievement at his feet, and his admirers awaited the new revelations.

A trip to Europe in 1889 had been of great benefit to Edison, enabling him to meet the great scientist Professor Marey, whose experiments with moving pictures involved not a cylinder, which had so far been Edison's guess, but paper-based film.

1889 is supposed to be the year in which Edison's assistant, W. K. L. Dickson, produced the first successfully projected moving picture, but historian Gordon Hendricks has gone into the matter with painstaking care and proved the claim pure fiction. Dickson did not even develop the Kinetoscope, a slot machine incorporating a moving picture loop, until 1892.

Out of respect for Edison's work, other inventors made their progress known to him. Some wrote or cabled direct to his laboratory. This was probably a form of self-congratulation, rather like a priest passing on his good deeds to the Pope. But in the case of British inventor William Friese-Greene, whose apparatus pre-dated Edison's, it was in the hope of a job. The information he enclosed was already common knowledge in scientific circles through its publication in *Photographic News*, February 28, 1890; Friese-Greene thought himself protected by a forthcoming patent. He was mistaken. Edison absorbed his ideas, but did not provide the job. And so the moving picture reached the public from the factory which had brought them the phonograph. Like the phonograph, it was contained in a box. Drop a penny in the slot, and a picture the size of a postage stamp sprang to life. Edison was always snobbish about the appeal of the moving picture, and he soon allowed other projects to absorb him.

Edison may not have invented the motion picture, but he did commercialise it, and in business terms that is almost more important. Many vital inventions have languished through lack of exploitation. Nevertheless, Edison had an influence on the moving picture out of all proportion to his real contribution.

By restricting the new invention to slot machines—placed in arcades just like phonograph parlours—Edison ensured a world-wide race to achieve projection. Edison himself, being devoted to the idea of machines in boxes, was anxious not to 'kill the goose that lays the golden eggs' by rushing into projection. Too many people would be able to see the film at once, and this would undoubtedly reduce profits.

However, on April 23, 1896, at Koster and Bial's Music Hall, New York, Edison demonstrated the Vitascope, a projector actually invented by Thomas Armat, who obligingly stood in the background, operating the projector, allowing, for the sake of commerce, all the credit to go to Edison.

The reactions to these first fragmentary films make delightful reading. The New York *Times* talked of "a buzzing and a roaring in the turret" when the hall was darkened. "The first picture shown," said *The New York Dramatic Mirror*, "was the Leigh Sisters in their umbrella dance. The effect was the same as if the girls were there on the stage; all of their smiles and kicks and bows were seen. The second picture represented the breaking of waves upon the seashore. Wave after wave came tumbling on the sand, and, as they struck, broke into tiny floods just like the real thing. Some of the people in the front rows seemed to be afraid they were going to get wet and looked about to see where they could run to in case the waves came too close."

Showmen, impatient with Edison's reluctance to market his projection machine, acquired machines of their own, partitioned off the rear portion of their arcade, and showed films on a screen. Then began the American public's love affair with the movies.

Thomas Alva Edison.

888

MG78804

The technique of film production on the rooftop studios was little different to the manufacture of lantern slides, with a few disadvantages of its own. The backdrops, hand-painted on canvas, and usually rented from a local vaudeville house, tended to shudder in the wind. Birds would occasionally land in shot—or worse. As soon as it rained, the camera and props would be rushed indoors, and the backdrop rolled up and stowed away. Strong sunlight was essential for a satisfactory exposure—showmen would reject dark and lifeless prints. Work would stop when the shadows crept up to the set—as seems imminent in this rare picture of the Lubin studio in Philadelphia. It is hard to believe the American film industry began in so haphazard a fashion.

128

The true source of power for the early film industry was the sun. Here is the studio of the American Mutoscope and Biograph Company in the course of construction, January 24, 1896. It is designed to revolve to follow the sun, on much the same pattern as the Edison 'Black Maria' studio—which is hardly surprising since the same man built it. W. K. L. Dickson (third from left, with arms folded), an Englishman, was a figure of outstanding importance, for he carried out Mr Edison's motion picture work, and must therefore be credited as the American inventor. He left Edison in 1895 and went over to the opposition, Biograph. He helped Biograph avoid the Edison lawyers by constructing a motion picture camera utterly unlike the Edison machine. He achieved this in partnership with Harry Marvin, E. B. Koopman and Herman Casler. The corrugated iron shed gives some idea of the immensity of the machine, which weighed five hundred pounds, and was brought from Canastota, New York to be installed by Dickson and Koopman in May, 1896. The studio was on the roof of the Hackett–Carhart Building, 841 Broadway, between 13th and 14th Streets, on Union Square, New York City.

The rooftop studios were a temporary phase, which provided just enough film to enable the manufacturers to sell the equipment to project it—for that was their primary concern. Once a chain of exhibition had been established, the demand for material far exceeded production. Film makers constructed proper studios— vast glasshouses, which admitted daylight but kept out the rain. Here were produced comedies and dramas, companies working side by side as long as daylight lasted. The Lubin Company, which began on the rooftop (see page 30), was soon housed in this glass studio in Philadelphia. It is similar to the Edison plant, but it is more dependent on natural light. (Artificial lights can be seen at the very back.) Only one company is working; on a busy day, several films would be in production, the sets put up side by side. The cameras have been placed to suit the still photographer. At this early date (around 1911), cameras would photograph the scene head on; a side angle like this would show more of the studio than the set.

The best equipped studio was that of the Edison Company, where daylight could be augmented by overhead Aristo arcs. In this picture, showing an elaborate stock-market scene of 1912, arc lights are also being used at the side of the set. The temperature inside those studios in summer was often unbearable, yet players had to obey convention and work in jackets and stiff collars. The Edison trademark can be seen on the rostrum, centre.

CHAPTER THREE

The Route to Respectability

Edwin Porter and the Theatrical Phase

WITH Edison preoccupied in the exalted realms of 'white magic', the industry needed a more accessible leader. The most popular contender for this title was Edwin S. Porter. He worked for the Edison Company, and his *Great Train Robbery* was responsible for taking the moving picture out of the slot machine era. He was an engineer; he developed cameras and projectors and special effect devices, and ultimately he preferred the world of engineering to that of film production. For Porter was not the dedicated film-maker that D. W. Griffith became. He enjoyed being an all-round film technician, cameraman-cum-editor like most film-makers of the time, but the fact that he developed the art of editing, and introduced many other refinements, was due more to his love of tinkering than his love for the medium. Having tried out ideas, he discarded them, perhaps feeling that he had proved what he had set out to prove.

As a film-maker, it was his respect for the theatre that finally set his style. As he wrote in 1914: "We must record the assertion that the development of the stage greatly assisted the advancement of the film, because even at an early date in the history of the industry, it was commonly recognised that the introduction of general dramatic principles in the production of motion pictures was desirable and necessary."

As an authentic pioneer, Porter is supposed to have helped install the Vitascope for Edison's presentation at Koster and Bial's Music Hall. But his career began in June, 1896—just too late. However, he did become a projectionist, and he once operated an advertising display on top of the Pepper Building, at 34th Street and Broadway. The advertising films, for Haig and Haig and Pabst beer, were enlivened with travel pictures, and the crowds became so vast that Porter was arrested. He worked for the Eden Musee, operating a projector which he designed and built himself. The Musee provided living picture backgrounds for their famous waxworks, and Porter had an unrivalled opportunity to study the films he showed. The films aroused more interest than the waxworks from the visitors, so the Eden Musee installed a large auditorium. Here Porter encountered the films of the French magician Georges Méliès, which he scrutinised with the utmost care, frame by frame. Thanks to his background as an engineer, he was able to break the code of Méliès's effects and took professional pride in concealing with a similar cloak of secrecy his own experiments.

Georges Méliès used the cinematograph to extend his act as a magician, and he produced a series of enchanting films, incorporating camera tricks and sleight of hand which can still astonish. Largely thanks to Méliès, the French cinema was more advanced, commercially as well as artistically, than that of any other country. Porter used his knowledge to emulate Méliès's work when he joined the Edison Company and became cameraman–director. His films around the turn of the century were considerably less ambitious than those of Méliès, but then the American cinema was still in the slot-machine stage, and a single scene was sufficient for penny-arcade patrons. (To tempt them to part with more money, arcade owners eventually ran several episodes in several machines; these were joined together for projection as soon as this was practical and became the first 'story' films.)

Porter made single-joke comedies, and such Méliès-inspired dramas as *Another Job for the Undertaker* (1901). *Uncle Josh at the Moving Picture Show* (1902) employed an optical printer, made by Porter, to show a character rushing up to the screen to help the heroine, and tearing it down as he tries to climb into the picture. It wasn't very skilful—when Josh's body crossed the screen, he became transparent—but it was fun, and the appearance of earlier Edison films on the screen was a technical feat. Intriguingly, the screen collapses on the operator, revealing a back-projection installation. Much more fitting for a student of Méliès was *Jack and the Beanstalk* (1902) which told a story, was graced with elaborate sets, and even involved the use of lantern slides. Hand-coloured prints of this subject have disappeared, but they must have been unusually impressive.

Fire was an omnipresent hazard in the early part of the century, when fire regulations were minimal and their enforcement virtually non-existent. One projectionist declined to show a fire warning slide on the grounds that it might cause panic among the audience, and he would have to pay for the damage. Fire was as common a risk for ordinary people as catching a cold; entire American cities had been destroyed by fire, and fire fighters were regarded as a very special breed. Several of the early films of Edison and Lumière showed fire departments answering an alarm, and the horsedrawn apparatus, belching smoke—an inspiring sight even today—quickly became a cliché. Nevertheless, such films were invariably applauded, as was a famous British film of 1901, *Fire*, which showed each stage of an alarm, and probably encouraged Porter to produce his *Life of an American Fireman* (1903). With its dissolves and its dream sequence, this film imposed the most dynamic elements of the stereopticon on the cinematograph; it became extremely popular, and ran longer than any other film.

Encouraged by the success of this little epic, Porter turned his company's attention to story films, and produced *The Great Train Robbery* in 1903. The most celebrated of all the primitive films, this subject was probably inspired by another British production, *Daring Daylight Robbery*, which was distributed in the United States by the Edison company (named after the Wizard rather than run by him) for which Porter worked. The rise of the American film industry was largely due to this one twelve-minute film. It has been copied so many times, and is shown today in such a pitifully fragmentary form that its original impact is hard to judge. A glimpse of an original 35 mm reveals it to be a thriller of outstanding showmanship. The pictorial quality is excellent, and the story clear and easy to follow; furthermore, painstaking effort was made in 1903 to hand-colour the film, just like a stereopticon slide. If it isn't entirely successful—the colour wiggles a bit—it doesn't obscure the excitement one still feels after all these years when the cash box is blown up, and the explosion registers as a red and yellow cloud; when the barn dance appears as a riot of reds, yellows and blues. There is excitement, too, in the locomotive hold-up scenes and the subsequent chase, even if the scenery, supposed to be that of the Far West, is all too obviously Eastern.

The link between motion pictures and the railroad companies paid handsome dividends throughout the silent era. The Delaware, Lackawanna and Western Railroad had launched an advertising campaign to emphasise the cleanliness of their line, thanks to the use of anthracite, and Edwin Porter had made them an advertising film. So delighted were the railroad people that they provided full co-operation for his production of *The Great Train Robbery*.

1903 is too long ago for anyone connected with its production to be alive. But in 1957, Paul Killiam and William K. Everson filmed an interview with the great western star, Broncho Billy Anderson, and he confessed to having applied for a job as a train robber. "Can you ride?" he was asked. "I was born in the saddle," replied Anderson. During the filming, he fell off his horse, and was given a more pedestrian role. "We made it all in two days," he recalled. "Then it was finished and taken to the reviewing room. After it was reviewed, they all looked up and they were dubious whether it would go or not. And Porter said, 'Well, the only way we can find out is to try it out in a theatre.' They tried it out first in the Eden Musee, on 14th Street, and we all went down to see it. They were all seated there, and the chairman came out and made an announcement; they were going to see something wonderful, *The Great Train Robbery*. The audience didn't seem to take to the idea very much, and then it started. They all started to get boisterous, and yell and shout 'Catch 'em! Catch 'em!' and different kinds of epithets, you know. When the picture was over, they all stood up and yelled and shouted 'Run it again, run it again.' So they did run it again, and then they wanted to run it again. Finally they turned on the lights and they had to put them out. And then on the outside there was a big gathering, that had got wind of it all, ready to come in again. I think they ran it for a couple of days.

"They then ran it to get the reaction of a better class of audience up at Hammerstein's at 42nd and Broadway. That was a vaudeville house. I was a little dubious about how it was going to go with that audience, which was a sophisticated, show-me type of audience. When the picture started they all started to get up as usual and walk out, but then turned back to look at it, and they all, slowly, as the picture went on, went back to their seats. And they sat there, stupefied. They didn't yell, but they were mystified at it. And when it was over, with one accord they gave it a rousing reception. I said to myself then, 'That's it. It's going to be the picture

business for me. The future has no end.' "

Porter's film may have been primitive, but that word gives the wrong impression, for it was pure cinema. It spawned a crop of imitations, like most successful films since. Sigmund Lubin made his own *Great Train Robbery* in 1904, and Porter parodied it with children in *The Little Train Robbery* (1905).

Yet with all his ability, *The Great Train Robbery* remained the summit of his achievements. After 1903, he settled for a series of straightforwardly dramatic productions which, with few exceptions, are without interest to a modern audience. Historian Jack Spears ascribes this to the fact that he spent so much time tinkering with inventions. But the Nickelodeon was anxious to please two audiences: the audience it had, for whom Porter produced social films such as *The Kleptomaniac* (1905)—a rich woman is pardoned for shoplifting, a poor woman is jailed—and the audience it wished it had, theatrical society. To discard the slum tradition and to duplicate the theatrical experience was regarded as the commercially sensible thing to do. It was therefore necessary to abandon tricks, which might render theatregoers irritated and impatient, and disturb the mood. Dramas were photographed from a single camera position, as though from the front of the stalls, with painted scenery and, wherever possible, stage actors performing in the grand, theatrical manner. Later on, actors were introduced at the opening of the film, in evening dress, bowing to the audience. A curtain would rise to reveal the first scene, and descend to close the story.

Porter did not entirely abandon his trick films—*The Dream of a Rarebit Fiend* (1906), inspired by Winsor McCay's comic strips, was something of a triumph, with a nightmare, induced by the consumption of Welsh rarebit, sending the hero hurtling out of the window and over New York, to be snatched up in a whirlwind of special effects and, after breathless adventures, to be deposited back in his own bed. But Porter was equally concerned with realism, as his social films showed, and the rest of the industry looked to him as a leader, as they would later look to Griffith. "He is the absolute master of his trade from beginning to end," said *Moving Picture World*. "He is perhaps the best qualified man to be in charge of a moving picture studio that there has ever been."

The studio Porter was in charge of, in 1912, was his own. He had left the Edison company 'for more money'; although he hardly had need of it, the sight of men with far less experience than himself, reaping huge rewards from the industry he had helped to build, drove him to become independent. Porter's photographs show a heavy-set, middle-aged man with a moustache; he seems a rather slow, dull kind of character. Far from it, according to *Moving Picture World*; "He is very hard on revolving doors and they spin like a top when he goes through. The fastest elevators are too slow for him and trolley cars are simply in the way. His full round face resembles a harvest moon, especially when he gets a good cigar, the clouds of smoke resemble an approaching storm through which the moon smiles benignly."

Among those who worked for him was Arthur Miller, later a great cinematographer. He remembered how Porter would often leave the set, when he was supposed to be directing, to attend to some device he had cooking in his mind, or in his workroom. The actors would discuss the scene, and when Porter returned, he would usually agree with them. "Porter was a director by necessity," wrote Miller. "He never had the ego to make a *great* director, or to be an actor. He was soft-spoken, kindly, completely unselfish, and always answered a question as briefly as possible, in order to make the other person think for himself. He never thought of himself as just a director. He thought of himself as a manufacturer of motion pictures, capable of handling personally every phase of film making, from turning the crank of the camera to printing and toning the final positives. His life was devoted to movies, and he did more to create the motion picture business than those who invented the camera."

Word came from London to Porter's Rex Company that the US rights to an extraordinary French production were available. The world's greatest actress, Sarah Bernhardt, who had recently made a farewell tour of America, had entrusted her performance as *Queen Elizabeth* to celluloid! Porter had a friend, an ambitious Nickelodeon manager called Adolph Zukor, who was fired by the idea of presenting full-length productions, in the European style, rather than the Nickelodeon menu of single-reelers.* Porter realised *Queen Elizabeth* would be ideal for Zukor, and they formed a new company, Zukor buying the rights for $35,000— an unprecedented sum. Knowing that the pillar of the theatrical establishment, Daniel Frohman, had recently been undermined by a series of flops, Zukor inveigled him into the company.

And so the Famous Players Film Co. came into existence, with Porter as Director-General. Porter, lacking confidence in his ability to direct great stage actors, suggested they hire someone with stage experience—"a fellow like Griffith". But Griffith had turned down a $50,000 a year offer to leave his company, Biograph, and had recommended Porter.

With his respect for the stage, and his deliberately theatrical style of picture-making, Porter was the ideal man in the ideal job. He was able to work quickly—with an engineer's efficiency, he made *The Count of Monte Cristo* in six reels in a couple of weeks, with the celebrated James O'Neill (father of Eugene) in the title role. He directed, photographed and edited it, and then found a rival concern, Selig, had pipped Famous Players to the post with another version of the same story. Zukor held back the release, but when it finally reached the public, the earlier film had done it no harm. It brought in a vast profit. *The Count of Monte Cristo* had nothing about it which might remind the audience of the despised 'galloping tintypes'. It was pure theatre, with just one close-up (of an object, not a person) in its entire length.

While it was easy to turn out these Famous Plays, it was not so easy to persuade the Famous Players to take part. Actors considered the movies another branch of streetwalking. Theatrical contracts warned that appearances would result in instant dismissal. Daniel Frohman had to convince his brother, Charles Frohman, not to blacklist the actors who worked in pictures.

* Vitagraph had pioneered this tradition with their dignified historical productions.

Sarah Bernhardt had made *Queen Elizabeth* from dire financial necessity. While the top American players were hardly in the same straits, money proved its usual irresistible inducement. James O'Neill had been seduced by the promise of twenty per cent of the profits. James K. Hackett only agreed to make *Prisoner of Zenda* when he was offered $1,250 a week and a part for his wife. Once on the set Hackett refused to do retakes, considering them an insult to his ability, yet he constantly stepped out of camera range. But Hackett proved a man of unusual perception. He began to take a genuine interest in the process of making a film and quickly realised that the emphasised representation of the stage needed to be toned down for the camera. He changed his mind about retakes and persuaded Porter to reshoot some of the earlier scenes in order to make them less exaggerated. What appealed above all to such actors was the chance of immortality on celluloid.

The Prisoner of Zenda, which Porter had rushed out first, cost more than *Monte Cristo* had grossed, but it was tremendously successful and brought in the missing audience in substantial numbers. The Famous Players in Famous Plays vision was now reality, and other Broadway stars signed, for equally huge sums. Feeling they had found the formula for success, Famous Players signed David Belasco and hired virtually all the Broadway cast of his play *A Good Little Devil*, including Mary Pickford. Porter filmed it, in the closest approximation of the original production; at the suggestion of his associate, J. Searle Dawley, he permitted the cast to speak their original lines, a flourish which could only have gratified those adept at lipreading.

Porter had now brought about the revolution in movie-going he had sensed so many years before. And having done the trick, he discarded it. Porter was now convinced that Zukor was importing the wrong stars. From a photographic point of view, Minnie Maddern Fiske and Lillian Russell were stout ladies, and Porter wanted Famous Players to develop their own young players. Returning from a trip to Europe, he found his authority at the company undermined.

"Edwin S. Porter was, I think, one of the most important men in the early days," said George Folsey, later an important cinematographer, and then an office boy at Famous Players. "But he was too interested in the technical end of it, and Zukor didn't understand that at all. I came into Mr Zukor's office and he and Porter were talking. Porter was objecting to the lack of authority he had now because of the new people coming into Famous Players. He was saying that he didn't have any authority at all, and couldn't even fire an office boy. Zukor said 'Yes, you can.' I thought he was going to say 'There's an office boy. Fire him.'"

If Porter's abilities were no longer prized by the business he had helped to found, it was because they were no longer unique. A whole echelon of clever technicians and skilled artists had taken their places alongside him. Just as Porter had studied Méliès, so they had studied him. More important, they had watched the rise of Famous Players, and decided that Zukor's approach made commercial sense. Several companies began trying out the Famous Players idea, importing Broadway stars and turning out theatrical productions. And some did it with more distinction than Porter.

The fun had gone out of making films, as far as Porter was concerned. He had lost his position as leader of the industry to D. W. Griffith. He didn't care for most of the stage stars he had to direct, and he had no skill with actors—a deficiency they no doubt made clear to him. Even on *Tess of the Storm Country* (1914) with Mary Pickford, he had been obliged to import the original stage director to show Olive Fuller Golden how to express the pains of labour. And Porter had no interest in administering a complex production programme. He might have left earlier, but he waited to sell his stock at a good price, which he succeeded in doing. Porter had already amassed a fortune. Now that he had no need to work again, he left Famous Players in November 1915, and took up his new responsibilities with the Simplex company, overseeing the manufacture of a projector he had helped to invent. Porter returned to his first love, engineering, or, as he would have put it, tinkering, never to be associated with motion picture production again.

Edwin S. Porter, an important pioneer, preferred tinkering with machinery to producing pictures. He made *The Great Train Robbery*, the film that ushered in the Nickelodeon era. By the time that era was over, so was Porter's career. He joined the Simplex company, and continued to tinker with machinery.

RUDOLF IN THE PRISON AT ZENDA = TO RESCUE THE KING

THE PRISONER OF ZENDA

James J. Hackett (right) in *The Prisoner of Zenda*. The set is well constructed, the interior is lit with artificial light, and the set-up is quite striking. Yet the overall effect is pure theatre.

right] The theatrical bias of Famous Players is clearly shown in this advertisement; unless one reads the small print, one might assume this to be a theatrical event. Frohman's name is prominent—while the film's director, Edwin S. Porter, is completely overlooked.

Daniel Frohman
PRESENTS
James K. Hackett

Words are as useless in describing the magnitude and massiveness of the production as they are in the picture itself! An expensive and extensive publicity campaign to make it your success as well as ours!

WILLIAM R. RANDALL

WALTER HALE

BEATRICE BECKLEY

FRANK COULTER

TOM CALLAHAN

JAMES K. HACKETT

MINA GALE HAINES

DAVID TORRENCE

FRANK SHANNON

More graphic, more comprehensive, more appealing than the original famous play. The tense story, combined with the imposing settings and the luxury and splendor with which the characters are surrounded, make this the film's greatest conquest!

And His Special Company in **"THE PRISONER OF ZENDA"** The tale of a man who was a KING, and a King who was a MAN, by Anthony Hope

IN MOTION PICTURES

Love and sacrifice—duty and desire—a vast, weak yearning smothered by the breath of Right—a lure conquered and a victory earned almost in the shadow of eternal defeat! And desolation, the soul's solitude, mingled with the wandering music of the world, combined in a sincere production and enhanced by the vigorous emphasis of James K. Hackett's romantic art.

COMMUNICATE AT ONCE FOR TERRITORIAL RIGHTS!

FAMOUS PLAYERS FILM CO.

Executive Offices, Times Bldg., N. Y. C.

Adolph Zukor, Pres.

Daniel Frohman, Managing Director

You cannot be too early — you may be too late!

CHAPTER FOUR

Guiding Light

D. W. Griffith and Biograph

IN the theatre, actors do not necessarily stop acting when they leave the stage. They develop an image, for it is through their impact upon other people that they ensure employment. David Wark Griffith began his career as an actor, 'Lawrence' Griffith. He intended to preserve the integrity of his full name until he had won success in his chosen field. His ambition was to write plays, and he had a low opinion of most of those in which he appeared. He came from the South, from Louisville, Kentucky, and felt he belonged to a class higher than the one in which he and his family found themselves. His father, a Civil War veteran, had an imagination which exceeded even that of his son. One of his fabricated stories of the Civil War so impressed his family that they inscribed it on his tombstone. 'Colonel' Griffith conjured up a family tree which led straight back to the ancient Princes of Wales. An intermediate ancestor was 'Lord Brayington', and for a time Griffith's stage name was Lawrence Brayington.

This fantasy, which seems so sad and trivial today, is a vital clue to the energy which drove Griffith to transform the motion picture. For Griffith, in the terms of his time, was a failure. He could not make enough money, either as an actor or a playwright, to sustain his fervent ambitions. For a time he lived in a New York flophouse, and his experience of poverty must have been a humiliating agony. It was in the hope of selling a scenario that he called upon Edwin Porter at the Edison Company in 1907, and found himself, instead, playing the lead in 'a German story' called *Rescued from an Eagle's Nest*, directed by J. Searle Dawley. It was a feeble picture, the very title destroying potential suspense. With its painted backgrounds intercut with location shots, it was an attempt to duplicate stock company melodrama which failed to please even the trade papers. "The boldness of the conception," said *Moving Picture World*, "is marred by bad lighting and poor blending of outside photography with the studio work which is too flat; and the trick of the eagle and its wire wings is too evident to the audience, while the fight between the man and the eagle is poor and out of vision. We looked for better things."

Griffith was more successful at the studios of the American Mutoscope and Biograph Company—Biograph for short—where he sold stories *and* secured parts. An indication of his quality as an actor was provided by cameraman Billy Bitzer, who was to accompany Griffith to the top of his profession; "My attention was directed to him because one day I was called on the carpet for having allowed him to be photographed in such a manner that he seemed to have three or four arms instead of the usual two. The fault was not mine, but his. He acted with so many gestures because, I later learned, that had been his stage style in costume dramas. The second time I encountered him, he overacted the part of the bartender, so in order to save myself trouble, I asked him if he was trying to get me fired, or wasn't he aware that his mugging was taking the action away from the lead? He confided that a friend had told him that was the way to act in pictures, but now that I had brought it to his attention, he wouldn't do it again." "That Griffith helped to eradicate this kind of playing from pictures is now well known," said the programme for *The Birth of a Nation*. "The old jumpy see-sawing of the arms and pawing of the air, misnamed pantomime, has disappeared under his watchful care."

Bitzer revealed that Griffith was put to work first on 'off-colour' pictures, for the Mutoscope. Poor Griffith; one can imagine how cast down he must have been by the experience. There was little demarcation between jobs in those days, and before long a director fell sick and Griffith was invited to replace him. Hesitatingly he agreed, on condition he could return to acting if he wasn't successful at directing. His first picture was to be *The Adventures of Dollie*, and one night he came round to Bitzer's home for advice on how to make it. Bitzer wrote a sort of continuity on the back of a laundry shirt-cardboard. (This set the style for Griffith's attitude to scriptwriting. Not even his monumental *Intolerance* had the benefit of a written scenario.)

For sixteen years, Bitzer and Griffith formed the industry's most rewarding partnership. The two men often stumbled upon 'innovations' by accident. At Fort Lee, Bitzer noticed a particularly attractive illumination on the faces of Mary Pickford and Owen Moore. He realised that it was reflected from the white gravel in front of them, and he shot a few feet. When he saw the effect, Griffith was delighted; Bitzer was so encouraged that he became even bolder and photographed scenes straight into the sun. One was such a disaster that the entire company had to spend a day making retakes—and in that era, a film could often be made in a day. Bitzer hastily added a home-made lens shade to his camera, and promptly created another problem; the edges cut into the picture area. But Biograph hailed this as another innovation. "They thought the shaded corners took away the hard, sharp edges," said Bitzer, "and added class to the picture."

The years at Biograph may have been years of experiment, but more importantly for Griffith, they were years of commercial success. Under his creative control, Biograph profits leaped. Griffith's rapid progress was largely due to the fact that he was a storehouse of knowledge of the popular theatre.

"Griffith had been an exceedingly bad actor," wrote Karl Brown. "It followed that he could be employed only by exceedingly bad producers at an exceedingly bad salary. He travelled the length and breadth of the country, appearing in turkeys of the rankest raw melodrama. This meant appearing before the cheapest of audiences, the great army of the unwashed, who paid ten, twenty and thirty cents—the familiar ten-twent'-thirt' price scale of the barnstormers of jerkwater towns and city ghettoes.

"Then, by a quirk of ever-unpredictable fate, these same town-and-country yokels became the audience upon which the nickelodeons depended for their life, liberty and pursuit of happiness.

"Griffith knew this. He also knew the psychology of the cheapest of cheap audiences as no New York producer ever could. Ten years of seeing audiences of the lowest caste go wild over the crassest of raw melodrama. What they wanted was a full-course theatrical feast of tragedy and comedy, not delicate tragedy but raw blood, and not witty comedy but blatant slapstick. Everything had to be spelled out in black and white; deep-dyed villains and the purest possible heroes and heroines."

As though trying to educate that public, Griffith provided first the raw melodrama, and then, unable to resist his poetic and artistic sensibilities, he would shade his characters, to make them a little more believable. Wry touches of humour and subtle moments of restraint were hailed with delight by the trade papers, but Griffith returned to the double-dyed villains with the next film. It was as though he made one picture for the more knowing audience in the cities, and another for those in rural areas. More probably, the subtly-shaded dramas were made for himself.

Under his direction, the Biograph players were kept hard at work, running over themes which were to be tried out again and again before the public. Griffith felt that the movies wouldn't last, that the lode should be exploited for all it was worth. When stuck for a story, he merely changed cast and costume and reshot an earlier one. His audience was soon as familiar with his favourite themes as he was with their delighted reaction to them. Their success led directly to his masterworks, and his brief period of pre-eminence in the American cinema.

The Biograph films were played by a stock company of skilful and attractive players, none of whose names were revealed to the public. (In England, they invented their own.) Biograph were determined not to land themselves with the theatrical star system and its fairyland salaries. The players might have sought alternative employment, with star billing, but their loyalty to Griffith proved stronger than their resentment at their anonymity.

"We'd been told by other people that we were very good," said Blanche Sweet, "that we were the best of all the companies. But all we knew was that we liked working for this man. We worked for Griffith, not for the Biograph Company. He was the one we wanted to please. If he came over after a scene was over and said 'that's good', that's all you needed. Just a small salary and his 'that's good'."

While Griffith was steeped in the traditions of the theatre, and in matters of morality remained essentially Victorian, the elements of his work which aroused admiration were those which were fresh and youthful, and which belonged expressly to the moving picture.

"I liked his short gesture for films," said Allan Dwan, a director with a rival company. "By that I mean his girls. They never made broad gestures. They were little gestures. They didn't make the wide, sweeping, old-fashioned theatrical movements such as we'd been getting from the old hams that came into the business. We all imitated him. We eagerly ran to the Griffith pictures to see what was new. His back lighting, with the aid of Bitzer, was magnificent. Nobody dared shoot towards the light. The sun had to be behind the camera, never in front. And his use of reflectors, throwing light back into the faces of people. The sunburst in the hair, the haloes on the girls, all those things were new and interesting to us, and all of us who had any sense copied him. So we regarded him as a leader, and I think the leader of our whole business. We've never had a leader since."

Griffith's Biograph films have been isolated as the only worthwhile productions from the pre-1914 period, but every era has its quota of outstanding films. Research for this series has uncovered more than we could use. While much of the Nickelodeon fare was primitive, many of the films were cleverly thought out, and expertly put together. Griffith was not the only man who knew the tricks of the trade.

But Griffith was a proud and ambitious man. He had entered the business when it was at its lowliest phase, not so much primitive as primeval. Such rules as there were he broke with lordly contempt, and the sparks that flew ignited a kind of passion in his audience. Whenever he enlarged his boundaries, he extended his audience's horizons. When he finished, he was the leader of an industry acclaimed not only as entertainment, but as art. It had not been an art when he joined it. Griffith did not achieve this miracle alone, but he deserves unstinting credit for achieving it at all.

There is something sad about this picture of the awkward-looking actor grimacing with his heavy make-up. One can almost sense how much Griffith disliked appearing in 'galloping tintypes', and how foolish they made him look. But this was how he began his dazzling film career; the picture was taken on the set of a Biograph film in 1908. A mere seven years later, he was to unleash the furies with his masterpiece *The Birth of a Nation*, which, however outstanding its artistic merits, would do nothing to improve life for the boy in the pram.

A rare picture of D. W. Griffith and Billy Bitzer on location for
Biograph around 1912. Bitzer is lining up a shot through ground
glass, which he has inserted into the gate—for there was no
viewfinder on the Mutograph camera. This vast machine, which
punched its own sprocket holes, was smaller and more portable than
Biograph's first cameras. Negatives made with it are still providing
superb quality prints. Karl Malkames—whose father, Don, once
worked with Bitzer—has converted a Mutograph camera to printer
and has rescued scores of original Biograph negatives.

A unique picture of Griffith at work in the Biograph Studios, New York, 1912. Griffith stands behind flowers. Another Biograph director, Dell Henderson, stands in shirtsleeves next to Bobby Harron (seated), with Mae Marsh next to him. In the background is Olive Fuller Golden. Charles Hill Mailes behind Harron, and, at far right, Christy Cabanne, a future director. Compare the faces of the actors with those of the technicians. Orthochromatic film registered skin tones much darker than they were in reality, and actors had to wear the heavy make-up which gives them, in stills, the look of the mortician's parlour. Some directors dispensed with make-up altogether, but the habit was not relaxed until the general acceptance of panchromatic film in the late 'twenties, and the introduction of incandescent lights. To this day, male actors often wear make-up for colour film and television.

In Griffith's autobiographical notes, he wrote: "I remember one day in the early summer going through the gloomy old hall of the Biograph studio, when suddenly all gloom seemed to disappear." His eyes had fallen on two young girls, Lillian and Dorothy Gish. He brought both to stardom, but while Dorothy proved a comedienne of great talent, Lillian became a great dramatic actress. Here is a rare photograph of Griffith together with his favourite star.

Lillian Gish writes: "I certainly look like a frump in that dress. Have no idea whether it was taken in New York or Hollywood, but could you burn my half of the photograph? And about those shoes . . . ???".

CHAPTER FIVE

A New World for a Nickel

Nickelodeons

FOR the working man, the railroad was a vital feature of life, either through direct employment, or because the tracks ran past his neighbourhood. Travel across the continent had given the immigrant the idea of the vast scale of the country, and because such travel was prohibitively expensive, a great hit of the 1904 St Louis Exposition was the Hales Tour, the brainwave of a Kansas City Fire Chief. He built reproductions of Pullman cars, equipped them with machinery to provide swaying, hissing and banging, and projected a film taken from a locomotive.

Hales Tours provided the spark of enthusiasm for a number of entrepreneurs, who became the most important producers in the business; Sam Warner of Warner Brothers, J. D. Williams of First National, Carl Laemmle of Universal and Adolph Zukor of Paramount.

When Zukor hit upon the idea of interrupting his Hales Tour and screening *The Great Train Robbery* in 1905, customers flocked to his theatre and he made so much money that he dismantled the Hales Tour apparatus and converted the theatre into a Nickelodeon. Other exhibitors, too, had found that Porter's thriller increased their turnover miraculously, and the Nickelodeon craze swept the big cities with gale-force intensity. By 1907, there were upwards of 3,000 of them. Pittsburgh could boast a hundred, Chicago 300, for all a man needed to break into the picture business was a projector, a vacant store and a few chairs. (The chairs were often rented from funeral parlours.) In warmer areas, you didn't even need a store. You set up your machine in the open, waited for darkness and opened the show. Such theatres were charmingly termed Airdomes.

Entertainment for working people was surprisingly varied. Apart from the saloon and the pool parlour, there was the boxing hall, the sports field, the amusement park, the 'ten-twent'-thirt' melodrama, the penny arcades, known as electric vaudeville, the burlesque, and the cheaper seats in such middle-class preserves as the vaudeville, the legitimate theatre, the opera and the concert halls. Add to this group the illustrated papers and the cheaper newspapers, which were compiled more for entertainment than for news, and it becomes apparent that ordinary working people were not deprived of opportunities for escapism and amusement. But the wages of this period—$5 a week was considered average—made people think hard before they spent money on entertainment. The Nickelodeon's 5-cent admission was not as cheap as it sounds, but it offered in one programme the same kind of fare as vaudeville, the same thrills as melodrama, potted culture from art galleries and the legitimate stage, action from the ballpark and boxing ring together with glimpses of foreign countries which could only be duplicated by travel. And on top of all this, topical items of sensational journalism, such as the Stanford White murder case.

The basic Nickelodeon (odeon was Greek for theatre) was a converted store, outside which, despite fierce local opposition, was often a phonograph and a barker, who shouted "only a nickel, five pennies, a half a dime!" At that price, few felt cheated. The Nickelodeon craze was regarded as easy money for entrepreneurs— another Klondike—and so it was, but because of the high rental offered to secure the site and wages for manager, doorman and operator, they were not cheap to run. To seat more than 200 required a theatrical licence, which cost $500 a year. Most Nickelodeons, therefore, seated 199, and paid amusement licenses at $25. A Nickelodeon had to have a weekly minimum of 4,000 visitors to cover the $200 running costs. Since by 1907, more than two million people were visiting Nickelodeons every day of the year, most of the little theatres were doing well. They weren't always so little, either. An exceptional Nickelodeon in 1907 was The Philadelphia; it installed 1,000 seats, paid its theatrical licence plus $35,000 in ground rent, and boomed.

Rural communities depended upon travelling showmen, although many villages had permanent theatres. The Nickelodeons, or Nickelettes, were centred in the urban areas. Proprietors had their eye on the middle class, and from the start, sites were selected close to middle-class shopping centres. Some proprietors were anxious to avoid too shabby a clientele for fear of discouraging their white-collar customers. Above all, they wanted women to attend— and some Nickelodeons tried charging them half price. It didn't work. Young women never attended the movies in large numbers until the picture palace era. Nickelodeons were not regarded as respectable, any more than the penny arcades. As late as 1913, no motion picture theatre was permitted within 200 feet of a church.

The Nickelodeon proprietors not only had to put up with class prejudice; at first there had been an understandable distrust of dark rooms. In Los Angeles, exhibitor Thomas Tally catered for this anxiety by erecting a partition fitted with peepholes, so that the customers might peer at the screen from the safety of his other attraction, a phonograph parlour. In the South, Nickelodeons experienced the restriction of the Jim Crow laws. Negroes entered the theatre from back alleys, sat in the balcony ('nigger heaven') of theatres large enough to have them, and were banned altogether from others—a ban which applied to many Northern theatres, too. There were also theatres for Negroes only.

For the first few years, each performance lasted only fifteen minutes and films were supplemented by song slides or lectures. As the Nickelodeon industry became more competitive, admission was raised to 10 cents; some shows lasted as long as an hour and the basic piano accompaniment was augmented or supplanted by a melodion. Interiors were usually painted red – a colour which inflamed reformers—and signs decorated the walls:
NO SMOKING, HATS OFF and sometimes

STAY AS LONG AS YOU LIKE.

People reacted with more feeling than we do today to popular entertainment. That is not to say they were more voluble—unless the film broke down. A 1907 account in the *Saturday Evening Post* described the rapt silence which greeted the films. There were virtually no subtitles to read out loud, or to translate into a dozen languages. Comedies were not accompanied by gales of laughter, but by suppressed giggles. The audience maintained a steady stare of fascination at the screen, and towards the climax, "lips were parted and eyes filled with tears".

Looking at the Nickelodeon films today, it is hard to imagine the intensity of feeling which they aroused, but before entertainment became as accessible as tapwater, people felt oddly flattered by public performances. One witness remembered thinking "all that trouble, just for me". The films themselves, in these early days, were equally naive. They were aimed at unsophisticated people (although they were no more naive than the commercials we see on television today). These little films formed the groundwork for the great classics of the silent era—the popular successes that would transform the industry, and the audience.

Billy Bitzer, with Mutograph camera, in Boston, 1898, making pictures for the American Mutoscope Company's chief customer, B. F. Keith, the Boston vaudeville tycoon. Keith had presented the Lumière programme in 1896—a series of short scenes from France which had introduced the European public to the moving picture.

Two years later, vaudeville still expected the same short displays of movement, such as a parade or a fire. One might imagine the cameramen being content to supply such scenes from their home territory. Far from it. Bitzer was sent straight from Boston to the Spanish–American war, in Cuba.

left] G. W. 'Billy' Bitzer, with the Mutograph camera lashed to the cowcatcher of a locomotive in Orange, N.J., making advertising films for a railroad company, around 1898. This is precisely the method by which the Hales Tour films were later to be made— the alternative being a shot from the observation car. Some of the Hales Tours were sponsored by railroad companies.

above] The only known photograph of a Hales Tour in operation — the picture on the screen has been superimposed. Copied from a trade magazine of 1908.

Byron Haskin, a future cameraman and director, saw a Hales Tour as a child: "The theatre was about fifty feet deep and the seats were on each side of a centre aisle, exactly like a railroad coach, with the same sort of rattan backs to them. The film was shot from the back end of a railroad coach going through the Andes. I sat there with a friend, another kid, and to us it was fairyland. We sat there all day looking at this scenic until we finally came to and they got us out to dust up. We went out and it was night. I'll never forget it. I got into trouble when I got home; my father had been looking all over the neighbourhood for us."

this page and previous pages] Four examples of early picture theatres, showing the kind of progress the exhibitors were looking for.

Thomas Tally's Phonograph Parlor (page 50) has been written about many times in film histories, but this is the first time I have ever seen a picture of it. The photograph was taken in 1897 at Tally's Phonograph and Vitascope Parlor at 311 South Spring Street, Los Angeles. The Great Corbett Fight refers to a boxing match staged at Carson City, Nevada between James J. Corbett and Bob Fitzsimmons, filmed by Enoch Rector's Veriscope, a special, wide-screen camera constructed for the occasion. This fight was tremendously popular among moving moving picture patrons, but it brought discredit upon the industry as a whole. "Until that picture appeared," wrote Terry Ramsaye, "the social status of the screen had been uncertain. It now became definitely low-brow, an entertainment of the great unwashed commonalty. This likewise made it a mark for uplifters, moralists, reformers and legislators in a degree which would never have obtained if the screen had reached higher social strata."

Page 51 shows a Nickelodeon in a rundown neighbourhood. Judging by the demolition, and the fact that the dentist next door has moved, the building itself is probably due to be torn down before long. Meanwhile, gaping windows are concealed with brightly painted signs; the price suggests the kind of programme you'd find inside—a fifteen minute show—for despite their name, most Nickelodeons charged ten cents for a full hour. Programmes, changing every day, ran from early morning until midnight. This is the kind of theatre that would attract police raids, for they would risk more suggestive subjects than their respectable rivals. The picture has been taken when women and children are in evidence . . . .

The third example (*above*)—Poli's Theatre, Waterbury, Connecticut about 1912—has also been taken to show that the clientele includes women and children. The difference is that these are middle-class women and children—the affluent family audience the Nickelodeon proprietors so craved for. Women and children were not a substantial part of the early audiences—in New York, they amounted to thirty per cent—but their very presence was a symbol of respectability. During the Nickelodeon era, important films like *Quo Vadis?* and *Traffic in Souls* were shown at legitimate theatres. While the movie industry needed the prestige of such theatres, it conducted a war against them. As the big picture palaces went up, many theatres closed down.

But there was internecine warfare, too. Producers of films needed guaranteed outlets. It was all very well to produce expensive pictures, but unless that picture could be shown in every city, it would never recover its negative cost. Adolph Zukor used strong-arm methods to gain control of theatres for Paramount. His representatives were familiarly known as 'the wrecking crew' or 'the dynamite gang'. His strategy won him control of the industry—and the attention of the Federal Trade Commission, which brought suit against Paramount in 1922.

On the right is one of Zukor's showcase theatres, Grauman's Million Dollar Theatre, Los Angeles, 1918. Such picture palaces provided a luxury undreamed of in the Nickelodeon days. The film is one of Cecil B. DeMille's marital comedies. Its star, Gloria Swanson, stands in the foreground.

53

CHAPTER SIX

Lawful Larceny

The Patents War

THE early years of the century echoed with the efforts of the Trust busters, for free enterprise was far too often a euphemism for racketeering. Trusts were groups of companies combining to pursue a common interest, and Trusts were illegal. The Sherman Anti-Trust Law and the Clayton acts were constantly being evoked against the 'rough stuff' of such magnates as oil tycoon John D. Rockefeller. Conglomerates collapsed, although their rulers invariably escaped the well-advertised jail terms, and set about rebuilding their empires.

The early days of the picture business were as tough and as dangerous as any gold rush, and to ensure survival you needed a lot more than a thick skin. War broke out for the usual reasons. One faction tried to stifle another; violence was the inevitable result. It was a colourful, often hilarious, but highly reprehensible period in the industry's development. It was called the Patents War.

Edison had neglected to register his Kinetoscope patents abroad—not considering it worth the money—with the result that the moving picture business in Europe progressed without the fear of reprisal that existed in America. Some first-rate apparatus began trickling into America. American manufacturers were themselves ignoring Edison's patents, and Edison blasted back at them with writ after writ. Unable to base a claim on the film itself, which was manufactured by Eastman, he did the next best thing and claimed the sprocket holes. No picture could move satisfactorily without sprocket holes, although flicker books provided the inspiration for a slot-machine, the main rival to Edison's Kinetoscope, the Mutoscope. With the help of Edison's former assistant, W. K. L. Dickson, the American Mutoscope and Biograph Company later invented an ingenious camera which used unperforated film, and punched the sprocket holes as it took the picture. The little squares of film fluttered to the ground from a pipe; combined with the racket of the hand-cranked machinery, the enormous Mutograph camera looked and sounded like a threshing machine.

While Edison's lawyers could take firm measures against the larger concerns, myriads of tiny operators could melt away at the sight of a writ like snow in the sun. On top of this, there was no shortage of entrepreneurs who would borrow or steal a camera, have its mechanism copied, and market it themselves. "A fourth of a producer's time and thought went to the making of pictures," wrote Benjamin Hampton, "and three-fourths were absorbed by legal battles with big and little competitors who sought to imitate his inventions or averred that he was stealing theirs."

Biograph was Edison's strongest adversary. Jeremiah Kennedy, a banker's representative from Biograph, suggested to Edison that they call a truce and pool their patents. Edison agreed, for despite all the legal action, the courts still allowed Biograph's camera. On September 9, 1908, appeared the Motion Picture Patents Company,

with Edison and Biograph as the sole stockholders, Vitagraph and Armat contributing their patents and gaining a cut, and a group of allies—Essanay, Kalem, Selig, Kleine, Lubin, Pathé (who left in 1910) and Méliès—as licensees. They each recognised Edison's Kinetoscope patents and submitted royalties for the right to use them. All of which must have amused Edison heartily, and afforded him a degree of revenge. For no basic part of the Kinetoscope was original with him. Edison despised the whole idea of patents, and it is hardly surprising that when he used them, he did so in an entirely self-serving way. "I have 500 patents," he wrote in 1891. "Not one was ever sustained. Law expenses $600,000. Patents have ceased to give any protection in this country. It's cheaper to steal them."

The patents office turned down several applications by Edison for moving picture devices, since other pioneers had already invented them. But one successful application, US No. 589168, gave Edison the power to overwhelm the smaller businessman, the so-called independent.

"You know what I call a good invention?" asked Edison. "Something so practical that even a little Polish Jew would buy it." This remark suggests an underlying desire on the part of the Patents Company—with names like Kennedy, Blackton, Rock, Marion—to keep the immigrant riff-raff out of the new industry. The independents, represented by names like Laemmle, Baumann, Dintenfass, were faced with a blockade; Eastman Kodak sold film only to the opposition. A licence fee, charged by the Patents Company, amounted to a mere two dollars a week; collected by the MPPC's distribution arm, General Film Company, it brought in the colossal sum of a million dollars a year. There were other royalties and agreements, establishing the MPPC so securely that the independent could only gasp at the effrontery of it all.

While the MPPC evoked the law, their case was based on fraudulent claims. But ethics in such a situation were as valueless as Confederate bonds. Strength was the sole essential. While the licensed companies touched their forelocks to Squire Edison, gaining their strength from numbers, the independents banded together in 1910 as the Motion Picture Distributing and Sales Company. They were wild with rage. The Patents Company was obviously a Trust, and the most arrogant example imaginable, yet because it had based its collaboration upon the common ground of patents protection, it was apparently legal. The independents nonetheless christened it the Patents Trust.

"All that its members had to do," wrote Benjamin Hampton, "was to sit tight, make movies, rent them at the highest possible price, and enjoy the profits."

Edison's ridiculous claim to the sprocket hole was upheld by no less an authority than the Supreme Court in December 1911, but the Court of Appeals reversed the decision in 1912, bringing untold joy to the independents. The court decided that, since Edison had not invented the film, he could scarcely patent the holes in it. Unfortunately, the court acknowledged that Edison *was* the inventor of the mechanism of the camera, and that decision sent the Edison people straight to the next most essential element after the sprocket holes—the loop. The necessity of the loop was beyond argument, for without it the film would simply break as soon as the camera was cranked. It was known as the Latham loop.

"They insisted they were responsible for the existence of the loop in the camera and they went to court and got an injunction," said Allan Dwan.

"We ignored it all and in order to stop us, they began to hire hoodlums to put us out of business—either by destroying the camera, if they could get hold of it, or by burning down our studios, if we happened to have one. That's one of the reasons most of us went to California, and to distant places, to get away from the packed areas where hoodlums could hide, appear with a gun suddenly and take away the camera. They found that by shooting holes through the camera, they could stop their use, and that became their favourite method.

"They sent gunmen out. In the area we were working, San Juan Capistrano, there was a railroad passing right by, and I thought it was unsafe to be that close to a main line, so I moved my company to a place called La Mesa, beyond San Diego. There, we had no fear of anyone sneaking up on us on a train, because we were watching the depot constantly. I had my three cowboys, the Morrison brothers, arm themselves with Winchesters, hire some other cowboys, and station them outside our area of work. So if anybody appeared carrying any kind of weapon, they were challenged by our people and disarmed.

"And so we were more or less secure. One day, a fellow got off the train, a sneaky-looking character, and asked to see the boss. I suspected him. I said 'Let's walk up the road a bit.' We walked up the road about a mile and came to an arroyo, a little stream running under a bridge, into which people had tossed a lot of tin cans. To impress me, he whipped out a side arm and fired at one of the tin cans in the arroyo. I immediately whipped mine out and fired. He missed his, but I hit mine three times. He turned round towards the depot and ran right into the three Morrison Brothers with three Winchester rifles aimed at him, and he decided it was about time to leave town. We were never molested again. The word got out that we were tough."

The use of gunmen was not exceptional. The battles between opposing unions claiming to represent the motion picture operators in Chicago featured gangsters, gunfights and full-scale riots. The circulation wars of the newspapers were equally violent. The Independents simply hired gangsters of their own to combat the Trust's gangsters, spies to match the Trust's spies, and lawyers to outwit the patent attorneys. But self-defence was costly. The Patents War contributed to the great exodus from New York and New Jersey.

There were some staunch individualists who refused to pay the $2 tribute to the Trust, as earlier Americans had refused the stamp tax to the British. But the Trust could crush them if it chose. Without licensed films, it was a brave exhibitor who depended upon the fitful releases of the independents.

Vigorous and morale-boosting opposition to the Trust came from Carl Laemmle's appropriately named IMP Company (Independent Motion Pictures), in splendidly scurrilous advertisements written by Robert Cochrane: "General Flimco's Last Stand" proclaimed a cartoon, depicting a beleaguered, moth-eaten general surrounded by Indians, his comrades labelled as Kennedy's brother-in-law, Kennedy's cousin, Kennedy's nephew. Laemmle must have seen himself in this position, however, besieged by a staggering bombardment of 289 lawsuits in less than three years. One of these gave him a solitary day in which to find an earlier use for perforations similar to sprocket holes; someone suggested a type of toilet paper which was advanced, like film, in a dispenser. The argument was upheld and Laemmle was saved.

As all movements seek a leader, so Laemmle, under whose name these advertisements appeared, became the leader of the independents. Communication was not easy, for film manufacturers were scattered as far afield as Maine, Florida, New Mexico and Oregon. IMP themselves spent several months in Cuba, although they were still pestered by Trust spies. Films made in distant locations were not always the result of flight—such locations were the fascination of the lecture hall, and Trust members exploited their audience value. Edison had a studio in Cuba, the Kalem company toured the Holy Land and Ireland and Méliès Star Film company embarked on a world cruise in 1913.

When the Motion Picture Distributing and Sales Co. split in 1912, and Pat Powers formed the Universal Film Manufacturing Company, Laemmle swiftly took control, and the internal friction created the flashpoint for a civil war. Universal behaved rather like the Trust itself. When the New York Motion Picture Company withdrew from the combine, the parent company set out to recover possession of what it regarded as company property.

"The Universal people hired gunmen to take the laboratory of the New York Motion Picture Company by force," said Irvin Willat. "My brother ran the lab. and told me we might have trouble, and he had got a couple of men to come over and act as guards. Well, between those two guards and the gang below trying to get in, there were five or six shots fired.

"They tell me Tom Ince lined up his cowboys at Inceville, and had a regular army waiting for them. I wasn't there to see that. But when I did go out West, we had another takeover attempt by Mark Dintenfass. I can remember distinctly Mr Ince called me and said, 'Irvin, take this .45, strap it on you and go down to the main gate. And if anybody comes you tell them they're not to get in. And if they try to get in, you have my permission to shoot them.' Mr Dintenfass and two others came down there. They knew me. They tried to talk me into opening the gate. I said 'Mr Dintenfass, my orders are to keep everybody out. I'm sure your intentions are honourable, but please don't come in or let anyone in because I'll shoot them.' And I think I would have. I wouldn't have that much nerve now, but I was in my early twenties then. And I kept them out. One of them said 'Well, I think the kid means it,' and they went away."

If both sides behaved equally badly in the Patents War, such behaviour was successfully kept from the public. On the surface, the Trust appeared to conduct itself in gentlemanly fashion. It explained its merger as an attempt to keep pictures 'pure', as a form of much-needed voluntary censorship. And it must be admitted that they faced so much corruption among exhibitors and exchanges that some studios were getting pitiful returns for their outlay.

From the beginning, the Trust pretended that they had no intention of monopolising the film business, that unlicensed exhibitors were free to use any film so long as it had not been licensed. But the most vigorous steps would be taken to prevent the indiscriminate use of both independent and licensed film. Those who raised their heads too high in this new profession risked more than their jobs.

Cecil B. DeMille, the director-general of the new Jesse Lasky Feature Play Co., had never made a picture before *The Squaw Man* in 1913, but his co-director Oscar Apfel was a former Edison man, well acquainted with the armoured strength of the Trust. Accordingly, they set out for Flagstaff, Arizona, an ideal spot to make a Western and the kind of town that might escape the notice of the Trust detectives. No one knows why they abandoned Flagstaff. Some say that it was raining. DeMille said in his autobiography that the weather was fine, but the terrain was wrong for the Wyoming background. Jesse Lasky Jr was told by his father (who remained in New York) that they ran into a cattleman–sheepman war, and a few bullets were flying round the station, so they got back on the train and kept going.

DeMille had packed a revolver in his luggage, just in case. Once he started filming in Hollywood, he acquired a wolf for a role in a picture, and kept it at his home. He should have kept it at the studio, for he found his precious negative unrolled into a heap on the floor, scratched, torn and worthless. Luckily, DeMille had shown the kind of resourcefulness that would bring him to the top of the business; he had two negatives photographed, and he kept one safely at home. Anonymous letters were the next stage of the attack; "Fold up your studio, or your life won't be worth much." He bought a larger revolver, and wore it conspicuously on his belt. For Hollywood in 1913 was a frontier town. Riding home one evening through Cahuenga Pass, he was shot at from the undergrowth, and sensed the bullet whistle past his head. The Trust was now shooting to kill, not just to immobilise a camera.

The Squaw Man company's next setback was their own fault. DeMille was apparently still buying unperforated stock, presumably because it was cheaper, for Edison's sprocket hole claim had been thrown out of court months before. A British perforator had been bought by DeMille at a bargain price, and it all but wrecked the film. As they found out later, the machine was not compatible with regular printers and projectors. At its first show the film dribbled its way through the gate, the picture sliding off the screen like a defective television. The Jesse Lasky Feature Play Company faced bankruptcy. Oddly enough, a member of the Trust came to their rescue—Sigmund 'Pop' Lubin of Philadelphia—whose technicians took the negative away and reperforated it. DeMille was overcome by the old man's kindness, and, unable to understand why he should have done this for a group of rebels, decided it was because he was "a good man". A charming, but unrealistic thought. Altruism was all but unknown in the war-scarred picture business. We may never know for sure why Lubin saved the Lasky Feature Play Co., but I offer a theory. Lubin was a notorious duper; he had duped, or copied, successful films and put them out under his own trade mark since the earliest days. He had remade *The Great Train Robbery*, shot for shot, shortly after the release of the original. Perhaps in testing the negative of *The Squaw Man*, his technicians were quietly pirating a print?

Apart from the attempted murder of promising new film-makers, what did the Patents Company achieve? It was guilty of the most arrant conservatism—stagnation would be a better description—in its business dealings. Money was pouring in, so the Trust considered the situation reasonably satisfactory. Apart from harassing independents, and forcing exhibitors to raise admission fees from a nickel to a dime, to squeeze out the little man, it was anxious not to change the status quo. The movies were, it felt, a temporary fad: 'let us squeeze the lemon until it is dry'.

It had forced film makers through sheer necessity to turn out inferior products, and to indulge in the most ridiculous precautions. Cameramen spent a great deal of their time under blankets, concealing the mechanism of their cameras from the gaze of bystanders. Cameraman Lucien Andriot remembered that his company, Eclair, received all their film without sprocket holes, and one employee spent all day and every day perforating film in the darkroom. These sort of practices scarcely encouraged the independents to the flood of experiment that this formative period so urgently needed. The creative energy went into survival and not into cinematic artistry. As Adolph Zukor put it; "They put some brains into their mechanical devices and into their sales department, but never by any chance into their films."

The Trust tried to win over Porter—of all the independents, Porter's Rex Company was the only one invited into the Patents Company—but Porter refused.

The Trust was initially opposed to the feature film, maintaining that a variety of subjects at a theatre was more in the public's interest than two long films, one of which might be a flop. The attention span of the Nickelodeon audience was brief, argued the Trust. And what about those who dropped in to the theatres with little time to spare, women who wanted rest after a tour of the shops—should they not be considered?

Not that the independents were united in their enthusiasm for the feature. Universal's Carl Laemmle was totally opposed to the idea, and *Traffic in Souls*, the company's first feature, was shown to him as a *fait accompli*. It took him some time to adjust to the fact that he had been presented with the richest prize of his career; *Traffic in Souls*, a story of the prostitution racket, was such a hit that people literally fought to get seats. The Nickelodeons would not accept features unless they were shown in single-reel episodes, so legitimate theatres were rented, and legitimate theatre prices charged.

Yet when George Kleine imported the Italian *Quo Vadis?* in 1913, he did not split it into single reels, but booked it into the Astor

Theatre at a dollar admission. Kleine was a member of the Trust, and he did it without the Trust's consent. It proved a historic event. Benjamin Hampton, a film producer and a chronicler of the industry, considers that *Quo Vadis?* began a new era in American film production and exhibition.

The strength of the Italian cinema lay in the apparently effortless expansion of its traditional operatic and theatrical spectacle into the new medium. The Italian epics were staged on a monumental scale, and, apart from their operatic acting, were often magnificent films. Their impressive length made the American one and two-reelers seem trivial by comparison. Griffith, who was always spurred to his best work by rivalry, embarked on a four-reel Biblical epic on Italian lines called *Judith of Bethulia* in 1913.

"It was a complete departure," said Blanche Sweet, the star of *Judith.* "We wanted to do longer films, and Biograph's answer to that was that people wouldn't sit still for longer films. You couldn't keep an audience interested. The front office wouldn't spend the money and it took Griffith two or three months to work it out. Making it actually took up a lot of time, because he had to build the high walls of Bethulia. I used to follow the action when I wasn't in a scene; I had a horse, and I followed him around when he was doing the battle scenes.

"Everything was on a much larger scale than he had ever used before. The battle scenes were longer, the vistas were longer, and he had so much more to make the film interesting and to make it hold. He had a beautiful story, of course, a tragic story, and that was against it. There had been tragedies before, but not too many of them. From every angle it was a risk. He was ready to take it, but Biograph weren't."

Judith was held up for release while Biograph negotiated with Broadway producers Klaw and Erlanger to make feature films, a programme from which Griffith was excluded. This so enraged him that he broke away from Biograph, abandoned New York and came to live and work in California, accepting an offer from Harry Aitken of Mutual.

The Trust was converted to the idea of features by the personal intervention of Zukor's theatrical colleague, Daniel Frohman. He won from Thomas Edison an impulsive commitment to the idea of Famous Players in Famous Plays and a letter asking the Patents Company to issue them a license. The Trust was then in an invidious position, obliged to license anyone with an ambitious and distinctive programme. The Trust began to lose power as it submitted to reason.

The independents' habit of poaching the Trust's employees, by the simple expedient of paying them more, was another factor in the crippling of the Patents Company. The slow process of law, which had driven impatient Trust members into using gangsters, was a further contributor to their defeat. The Patents War fizzled out as the independents, spearheaded by Universal, slowly ground the Trust to dust in the courts. Officially prosecuted under the Sherman Act, the Patents Company was eventually unmasked as a Trust, and was ordered to dismember itself by the United States government.

The outcome of the Patents War—and a very important outcome —was the firm establishment of the star system in American films. The Trust had not stifled its own stars—Vitagraph had introduced two of the earliest with John Bunny and Maurice Costello (top of the first popularity poll in 1912), and Francis X Bushman had a great following at Essanay—but they preferred to subordinate the players to the brand-name of the company that made the film. The public, however, found it easier to fall in love with people rather than companies. The independents knew how to manage the star system. And those simple facts helped to break the hold of the Trust.

Cameraman Irvin Willat with the IMP Co. (Independent Motion Picture Company) attempting to escape from the Patents Trust by fleeing beyond the range of American courts to Cuba. (Oddly enough, the Trust was waiting for them, as the Edison company already had a studio there.) Willat photographed several Mary Pickford films in Cuba for director Thomas H. Ince, and sometimes kept a loaded .45 on top of the camera in case of trouble.

left] Allan Dwan at the wheel of a De Lannay Belleville automobile, California, 1911. Roy Overbaugh, cameramen, extreme left.

The Centaur Film Co. opened the first studio in Hollywood in 1911—calling it the Nestor studio—and Horsley and Rosher were both part of it. They were English; the Horsley Brothers were the business heads of the enterprise, while Charles Rosher was a cameraman (he became one of Hollywood's greatest, with such films as *Sunrise* to his credit). Nestor formed part of Universal, which under the energetic leadership of Carl Laemmle, did much to destroy the Trust. Bill Horsley evidently felt sentimental about the old store which formed their humble origins—but he had it photographed too late. It was by now a Salvation Army post, and 'Centaur Film Co' has been painted on the negative.

CHARLES ROSHER *from* BILL HORSLEY

In this building at 900 Broadway, Bayonne, New Jersey, twenty-two feet wide, fifty-two feet long, on a lot one hundred feet long by twenty-five feet wide, David Horsley started making motion pictures in 1907 under the name of Centaur Film Company. When the Motion Picture Patents Company was formed in 1908 every single company in the U. S. was allowed to join except the Centaur Co. "They only had a wash tub and a sink", was the excuse for refusing a license. This then became the **birth-place** of the independent motion picture industry of the United States, and in five years time it became so big that it killed the **trust** which tried to strangle it in the place where it was born.

Judith of Bethulia (filmed 1913, released 1914) was D. W.
Griffith's first attempt at an epic on the scale of the Italian
pictures. It was imaginatively and impressively conceived, but
the Biograph management opposed such reckless spending.
They were not interested in long films, while Griffith felt
stifled by the limitations of one- and two-reel pictures. The
final cost was 100 per cent over budget, and Griffith was
carpeted by the heads of Biograph. They appreciated his value
as a director, but insisted he abandoned control of expenditure.
Instead, Griffith abandoned Biograph, and the company never
amounted to anything again. Ironically, they added two reels of
out-takes and reissued *Judith* in 1917 as *Her Condoned Sin* in six
reels. Lilian Gish, centre-right. (Frame enlargement.)

CHAPTER SEVEN

The Mesmeriser

Griffith's Masterpieces

IN other arts, millions are expended to preserve a work in its original state. In the movies, the money is spent to *prevent* the film remaining in its original state, because that state is highly dangerous. It is therefore hard to judge the true value of the films of the silent era, since copies are generally travesties. This is particularly true in the case of D. W. Griffith. Not only has the delicate quality of the photography been debased; Griffith's own attitudes have become so archaic that his work is greeted today as much by laughter as applause.

Nevertheless, it is a tribute to his genius that seventy years after he began work as a director, his major films are still regarded as masterpieces. Griffith himself is still regarded as the innovator of the language of film. So much has been written about him, however, that his work has been submerged by praise, and the expectation of an audience for a Griffith film is thus unnaturally high. Few artists, however talented, can retain their reputation through generation after generation—and in an art subject to such violent change as the motion picture, the mortality rate for genius is high.

To appreciate what Griffith did without romanticising his achievements, it is necessary to strip some of the legends away. Like Edison, Griffith was blessed (or cursed) by the talent of top-flight press agents. They conducted their campaigns in a curious manner, treating their subject with the kind of reverence usually reserved for the deceased. They poured into their advertisements quotations one might see carved on a statue: "The most sane and imaginative American who ever revolutionized the theatre when it needed an emancipator." . . . "He has far exceeded the power of the written word. It would be impossible for the greatest master of language to picture the emotions as Griffith has perpetuated them." . . . "D. W. Griffith is the Creator of the Eighth Art of the World!"

The campaign was mounted when Griffith left the Biograph Company, with the publication in the *New York Dramatic Mirror* of a celebrated advertisement: "D. W. Griffith, producer of all the great Biograph successes, revolutionizing the Motion Picture Drama, and founding the modern techniques of the art. Included in the innovations which he introduced and which are now generally followed by the most advanced producers are: the use of large closeup figures, distant views, as reproduced first in 'Ramona', the 'switchback', sustained suspense, the 'fade-out' and restraint in expression, raising motion picture acting which has won for it recognition as a genuine art."

Although the word 'introduce' is marginally less arrogant than 'invent', Griffith was not responsible for the close-up or the fade-out nor would it have made the slightest difference if he had been. What counted was how such devices were used. Griffith used them efficiently, sometimes brilliantly, and the tendency is to credit him

with everything possible in the cinema. The trouble is, that by piling all these offerings on Griffith's altar, one obscures the true object for admiration: the quality of Griffith's direction.

The travelling shots, the dynamic editing and the colossal sets are all incidental beside this element. It is not always apparent. Some of Griffith's films—*Home Sweet Home* (1914), *Dream Street* (1921)— are completely lacking in any sign of outstanding direction. But take the scene in *Orphans of the Storm* (1921), when Lillian Gish hears the distant voice of her long-lost sister, begging in the street below. Griffith holds Lillian Gish's ethereal face in close-up; her blonde hair is illumined by a halo of light. The electricity between Griffith and Lillian Gish is so hypnotic that the audience finds itself straining to catch the merest movement of an eyelash. Miss Gish hesitates, moves her head slightly—"no" . . . one can see her dismiss the thought . . . "that cannot be my sister". But the voice reaches her again. Her eyes flash with wild hope, then the lustre fades as she attributes the sound to her imagination. When the voice recurs, and she realises she is not mistaken, the tears well in her eyes—and in ours. One reaches the climax of the scene sharing with Lillian Gish a sense of love and desperation instilled by direction of brilliance.

All his other achievements are overshadowed by this ability to transfer to a length of celluloid the most poignant degree of emotion. Here is something which *can* survive the centuries. However skilful the other early directors might have been, none of them knew how to project anything but the most basic emotions until Griffith showed them. And it was emotion, rather than close-ups and fade-outs, that made the people of the world fall in love with the moving picture.

*   *   *

A remarkable find by the newly formed American Film Institute occurred in the late 1960s. They discovered that D. W. Griffith, in 1930, had made a short talking prologue to his sound reissue of *The Birth of a Nation* (1915). It took the form of an interview between Walter Huston and himself, and it was intended to explain the background to *The Birth* for a new generation which had never seen it. In the interview, Griffith explained very little about the film. He talked movingly of the Civil War, and Pickett's Charge, but when it came to revealing the secrets of his masterpiece, he was strangely reticent. "I don't think I deserve the credit," he said. "It was a story *about* something. Anyone could tell that kind of story."

The little film, lost for forty years, revealed something very important about Griffith. It captured with fidelity the quality of his voice. Every actor directed by Griffith has acknowledged the power of his voice, and one can understand why, simply by listening to this film. In a dramatised moment, when Huston presents

Griffith with a Civil War sword, one can see the ham actor in Griffith come to the fore. "Truth," he says, inserting a significant pause. "What *is* truth?" And when Huston demands the traditional coin in return for his sharp gift, one can see the charm of the man. "You don't care what you do with my money, do you?" he laughs.

This fusion of artifice and spontaneity is characteristic not only of Griffith himself, but of his films. There are moments of insufferable hokum and embarrassing coyness in his work, but the sheer love he shows for the cinema, for the people in front of the camera and for his subject, invariably triumphs. While his Biographs are often his most satisfying, the work he did when he left Biograph is considered his most significant. Since the list includes such titles as *The Birth of a Nation*, *Intolerance*, *Hearts of the World*, *Broken Blossoms*, *Way Down East* and *Orphans of the Storm*, one can hardly deny that the period from 1913 to 1922 was his most influential.

The Birth of a Nation is one of the key films of motion picture history because it brought pride of achievement to Hollywood; furthermore, it caused such controversy that everyone had to see it, and it broke through yet more of the prejudice against pictures that existed among the middle classes. It was packed with cinematic ideas, most of them developments from the Biograph films. These ideas have become absorbed into the technique of film making, and the picture doesn't surprise anyone today, particularly when it is shown in an eye-straining dupe, nearly twice as fast as intended. But when the American Film Institute found the Griffith interview, they also found an original toned print of *The Birth*. After sixty years, it was at last possible to appreciate the grandeur of much of Billy Bitzer's photography, and thus to penetrate to the spirit of genius behind the direction.

The Birth was adapted from Thomas Dixon's novel and play *The Clansman*, which dealt with the experiences of a family during the Civil War and the Reconstruction. To describe the novel as a repellent piece of work would be flattering it; that Griffith could transform such material into a masterpiece was as astonishing as the dynamic way he did it. The idea of mounting a massive spectacle on the slender resources offered by Harry Aitken was foolhardy enough. As production costs exhausted the budget Griffith began to seek money in the least likely places.

"Two men collared Bitzer outside our camera room," recalled Karl Brown, who served as Bitzer's assistant cameraman on *The Birth*. "One was Harry Aitken, and the other one was J. A. Barry, who seemed to be a manager of sorts. They wanted to borrow ten thousand from Bitzer. 'Well,' Bitzer said, 'you can have the money. I don't care. It isn't doing me any good. But it's four o'clock now, the banks are closed. I'll get it for you in the morning. How's that?' They said, 'You can get it for us now'. He said, 'You can't get in, the bank's closed.' Aitken said, 'We'll open it.' They hustled him away, and that's how Bitzer happened to invest seven thousand dollars. His share was somewhere in the region of ten per cent of the profits of *The Birth of a Nation*, which was to gross about five million dollars."

The Birth of a Nation was not the first film on the Civil War. Griffith himself had tackled the subject in such films as *The Battle*, and Thomas H. Ince, whose studio occupied a vast area of Santa Monica, had staged some brilliant reconstructions of Civil War engagements in films like the five-reel *Battle of Gettysburg* (1913, directed by Ince and Charles Giblyn). Ince's films, for sheer action and spectacle, were virtually impossible to outdo. What Griffith planned was a saga—a long story about members of a family—rather than an epic, which was the narrative of a hero.

Playing the leads were all the Biograph favourites—Lillian Gish, Mae Marsh, Henry B. Walthall—with the exception of Blanche Sweet, who had left to join Famous Players–Lasky. And forming the basis of the story were all the tried and true Biograph situations, most of which were familiar to audiences of melodrama. Griffith depended not on innovation to sell *The Birth*, but familiarity.

The Civil War had occurred only fifty years before; as the most catastrophic event in American history, the subject still aroused more passion than nostalgia. *The Clansman* had proved its popularity as a stage play over the years, but *The Clansman* was only the springboard for Griffith's enthusiasm. Although he had been born too late for the war, his father had told fantastic tales which had deeply impressed him as a child. He had been steeped in the subject, in the South's defeat and humiliation at the hands of the invaders. He saw this new film as a God-given opportunity to tell the world how the South had suffered, and how, thanks to a guerrilla army known as the Ku Klux Klan, they had fought back and won a kind of victory from defeat.

During the production, which began, appropriately enough, on July 4, 1914, war broke out in Europe, giving the picture a useful topicality; the mood in America being isolationist, Griffith ensured that however exciting the battle scenes, their grim result was also shown.

Griffith was in exuberant mood when he started shooting. "The first scenes we took," said Karl Brown, Bitzer's assistant, "had to do with an election and a negro dance. Well, when those negroes started dancing barefoot on the dry ground, kicking up clouds of dust, clapping their hands, their banjoes ringing, Griffith, who was back of the camera, was emotionally in that scene and was having a wonderful time."

The battle scenes were staged near Griffith Park (named after the Colonel Griffith who donated it to the city, no relation to D.W.).

"That was a case of the most careful kind of preparation," said Karl Brown. "The kind of preparation that military commanders should do for their real battles, but do not. Every gun emplacement was known. Every motion of every section of the crowd. I say section, because each section was put under a sub-director—one of Griffith's many assistants—Victor Fleming, Joseph Henabery, Donald Crisp. Name a roster of great directors, and they once worked with Griffith. They had what were called units scattered on both sides of the parapets of the Confederate and the Union. They were handled not by megaphone, because the megaphone could never be heard over the noise of battle with blank cartridges, but by a series of flags—red, white, yellow, blue, pink—which could be waved in a certain direction. If he wanted more action out of one side or another, or more action in between, that could all be done by flag motion."

The battle was revealed in a vast long-shot, photographed from a hill. The violent explosions were the responsibility of a one-armed pyrotechnician called Fireworks Wilson.

"Now having only one arm, and having to handle all these explosives, he used a professional fuse, the kind that spurts fire. It doesn't glow like a punk stick. He had a Mephisto moustache and beard, and wore this fuse between his teeth with the fire spurting out, and he was always asking questions. The explosives were under his good arm, their fuses hanging forward, and the fire getting closer and closer. Of course, we all drew back with unanimous consent. He said there was never any danger, he'd never had an accident in his life, but the silent witness of the stump convinced me it had not been nibbled off by mice, I can tell you that.

"Just outside the range of the camera, a number of men with good throwing arms were positioned to throw in a hand grenade, made with black powder, black sawdust and a fuse.

"Now the fuse ran out through the top, and it could be lit. You watched that fuse; when it got to the point where it was disappearing, then you threw it. As Fireworks Wilson explained, you must throw it at exactly the right moment; if you threw it too soon, all you got was a wiggly white trail from the fuse. While if you threw it too late and it exploded in your hand, why, it might hurt a little."

The military material was mostly rented; the muskets were hired from Bannerman's, in New York. Cannon presented a problem; they were used as memorials in the East, but the Civil War was not fought in the West, so Frank Wortman, Griffith's construction man, had to build them.

"As soon as it became known that we wanted horses, we had them, because we lived in the land of the cowboy and his bronco," said Karl Brown. "The Klansmen had to be clad in white from head to foot, and so did the horses. We transported them to a place out of town called Del Monte, near a stream called the Rio Hondo, so we had rivers to cross, we had lanes to ride in, we had hills. We didn't know exactly where these rides were going to cut in, so we took them riding along the sky line, we had them riding down hills, and we had them splashing across rivers. Both ways in each case.

"There was only one episode in all this riding which bothered me. Griffith decided that he wanted to get some sort of an effect of these hoofs coming right at the audience. Well, I was only a camera assistant. I didn't amount to very much, so I was expendable. I was put down with my camera squatted with its legs flat out. I was lying flat at the back of this Pathé camera, which turns from the rear, right next to the platform where Bitzer was getting the usual high shot. I thought this might be a little risky, but the cowboys told me that a horse will never, never run over anyone if there's any way he can avoid it. Well, there was no way to avoid it this particular time because these white covers we had on the horses got bunched up until they nearly knocked over the platform. Instead they jumped over me and everything would have been fine except the rear hoof of one of the horses hit the front magazine and sent it spinning. Film was running out of it like ribbons from a magicians hat. Fortunately, it was the front magazine—the unexposed film—so the shot was saved."*

* Sadly, the shot never made it to the final prints.

64

Take away the crowd scenes, and any of today's home movie enthusiasts could duplicate the conditions under which *The Birth of a Nation* was made. Infinitely more labour-saving devices are at his fingertips than were available to Griffith and his cameraman Billy Bitzer. They used no lights—Bitzer employed mirrors to bounce the sun around. There were no exposure meters or zoom lenses or lightweight cameras. Just a heavy wooden Pathé, sturdy and well designed, cranked by hand. Yet photographically it was outstanding, and the direction was often inspired.

Lillian Gish had suggested to Griffith during production that the scenes with the Klan, and the explicit racial elements, might cause the picture to be stopped. "I hope to God they do stop it," replied Griffith. "Then you won't be able to keep the audiences away with clubs!" He undoubtedly recalled that Dixon's play had sparked riots in 1908.

Despite this brutal remark, Griffith was probably as surprised as anyone at the power of his film. "The fact that the showing of *The Clansman* started riots and put blood on the streets," said Karl Brown, "was proof beyond proof that it was a great and powerful picture. Regardless of what any critic might have to say about it, the proof was there."

The praise from the established press drowned for a while the noise of protest; the picture was presented in New York with all the prestige of a legitimate theatre (the Liberty) and the associated high seat prices, just as Griffith had dreamed. It ran for forty-four weeks. And the chorus of praise was beyond his wildest hopes. "Only a genius could have conceived and produced such an inspiring spectacle," said the *Chicago Daily News*. "A new epoch in the art is reached" (*New York Herald*). "Never before has such a combination of spectacle and tense drama been seen" (*New York Sun*).
"Beyond doubt the most extraordinary picture that has been seen" (*New York Globe*).

Novelist and future film maker Rupert Hughes wrote a tribute in which he said he came from the film feeling "I have done the South a cruel injustice." Perhaps no greater praise was possible for Griffith, which explains why he reprinted Hughes's paean in the programme. Hughes continued:

"There has been some hostility to the picture on account of an alleged injustice of the negroes. I have not felt it; and I am one who cherishes a great affection and a profound admiration for the negro . . . *The Birth of a Nation* presents many lovable negroes who win hearty applause from the audiences. It presents also some exceedingly hateful negroes. But American history has the same fault, and there are bad whites also in this film as well as virtuous. It is hard to see how such a drama could be composed without the struggle of evil against good. Furthermore, it is to the advantage of the negro of today to know how some of his ancestors misbehaved and why the prejudices in his path have grown there. Surely no friend of his is to be turned into an enemy by this film, and no enemy more deeply embittered. *The Birth of a Nation* is a chronicle of human passion. It is true to fact and thoroughly documented. It is in no sense an appeal to lynch-law. The suppression of it would be a dangerous precedent in American dramatic art."

But suppression was what the opposition demanded. Despite appeals that the story was authentic in every detail—author Dixon proclaimed that he would never have allowed anyone but the son of a Confederate soldier to direct the film of his book—the Mayor of New York was assailed by protests. He ordered the License Commissioner to cut some of the most offensively racist material. No one will ever know exactly what that material contained, but Francis Hackett, in *New Republic*, supplied a clue: "The drama winds up with a suggestion of Lincoln's solution—back to Liberia—and then, if you please, with a film representing Jesus Christ in 'the halls of brotherly love'." About 500 feet were lost—although many cuts were the result of Griffith's attention to audience response.

The criticism wounded Griffith, for it emanated not only from the National Association for the Advancement of Colored People, but from such distinguished men and women as Jane Addams of Hull House; Dr Charles Eliot, President of Harvard; Eugene Debs, the socialist leader; Oswald Garrison Villard; and Francis Hackett, drama critic of the *New Republic*. They demanded the complete suppression of the film, despite the fact that some of them hadn't seen it. Blacks found it hard to see in any case, for many theatres refused to admit them. "*The Birth of a Nation*," said Anita Loos, who worked for Griffith as a writer, "created a racist problem in the United States that exploded and caused any number of theatres to cancel the film, and this horrified D. W. Griffith, who had been raised in the South, and who saw nothing wrong in it at all."

Compared to Dixon's original, Griffith's racism was mild. *The Clansman* read like a tract from the Third Reich: ". . . for a thick-lipped, flat-nosed, spindle-shanked Negro, exuding his nauseous animal odor, to shout in derision over the hearths and homes of white men and women is an atrocity too monstrous for belief." Griffith used none of this. Yet what remained was still alarming. *Uncle Tom's Cabin*, as a book, carried such enormous political impact that it helped to start the Civil War; the film versions were not watered down, but they were bloodless by comparison.

The opposition to Griffith's picture sprang from the fact that it made full use of the medium—and the medium proved too powerful. *The Birth of a Nation* remains a highly inflammatory piece of propaganda; it cannot be shown publicly today without causing enormous offence to the black members of the audience.

The trouble surrounding *The Birth* has undoubtedly been exaggerated—*Moving Picture World* reported 'a small riot' in Boston. The blast and counter-blast made news, however, and brought into the theatres not only the regular motion picture audience, but people who had never attended before.

Griffith wrote a pamphlet called *The Rise and Fall of Free Speech in America* in which he declared, "The right of free speech was bought at the price of blood" and "Suppression of motion pictures implies suppression of the press." The temperature of the argument suggests how deeply Griffith had been hurt. Each page was illustrated with a cartoon, and statements in bold type; on the back was the small print. The heading, repeated throughout the book, was significant; INTOLERANCE—the root of all censorship. INTOLERANCE—crucified the Christ. INTOLERANCE—smashed the first printing press. INTOLERANCE—invented Salem witchcraft.

Yet, ironically, it was intolerance which kept *The Birth* on the screen. The NAACP had launched its campaign in the belief that, however fine a film *The Birth* may have been, people were more important than pictures. Rev. Thomas Dixon, according to his biography, conducted his own campaign among the powerful of the land. He showed the film to the President, "It is like writing history with lightning," quoted Woodrow Wilson, whose enthusiasm won Dixon a meeting with the Chief Justice of the Supreme Court, Edward White. White was an intimidating man, and Dixon lured him to see the film by telling him of the President's reactions.

"You tell the true story of the Klan?" asked White.

"Yes—for the first time".

'He leaned toward me and said in low, tense tones: "I was a member of the Klan, sir. Through many a dark night I walked my sentinel's beat through the ugliest streets of New Orleans with a rifle on my shoulder. You've told the true story of that uprising of outraged manhood?"

"In a way I'm sure you'll approve."

"I'll be there!" he firmly announced.'

With evidence that the President and the Chief Justice both approved of the film, the NAACP found suppressing it extremely difficult. However, it was banned for ten years in Kansas, (the ban was actually lifted in 1923) and also in Chicago, Newark, Atlantic City and St Louis. The President's advisers were forced to deny that Wilson had endorsed the film, and to cap the contradictions, the Grand Army of the Republic charged that the picture was unfair to Union soldiers. It objected to the explicit scenes of rapine and pillage indulged in by the Northern forces, both black and white. Most ironically of all, *Moving Picture World* reported in September 1915 that Negroes were applauding it. In the South, said a S. Carolina historian, a carnival atmosphere reigned whenever the picture came to town.

The most depressing fact to emerge from the tumult was the revival of the Ku Klux Klan. This organisation, which Griffith himself admitted had spilt more blood than at Gettysburg, had disbanded in 1869. The modern Klan began its clandestine cruelty on Thanksgiving Night, 1915, on Stone Mountain in Atlanta, where, in June, 25,000 former Klansmen had marched down Peachtree Avenue to celebrate the opening of the film. Historians who cannot bring themselves to admit the connection, insist that the KKK did not achieve its greatest strength until the 'twenties, and the part played by the film remains in dispute. However, a quick comparison between the advertisements for the film and those for Klan recruits will dispel all doubt. The organisation was to have been called The Clansmen but it reverted to its original name. It gathered tremendous force in the 1920s, and its influence still darkens the South.

Meanwhile, Griffith was already at work on his next enterprise, *Intolerance*. In three hours and four stories, *Intolerance* carries not the barest hint of the fiercest intolerance of all: race hatred.

The Birth of a Nation provided the Ku Klux Klan with the finest possible publicity for its revival in 1915. The organisation was to have been called The Clansmen. The similarity between these two advertisements is self-evident. But whereas the film used a few hundred extras and made claims to 18,000, the membership of the Klan multiplied alarmingly. By the mid-'twenties it reached four million and they could stage rallies and marches which were not outdone for sheer scale until Nuremberg.

D. W. Griffith, (foreground), Billy Bitzer (right), Karl Brown, during the making of *The Birth of a Nation*. Said Karl Brown of this picture: "Bitzer was under the impression that heat on the magazines affected the film, so he rigged a sort of radiator consisting of a hollow shell to fit over the magazines. This shell was filled with water, and the corrugations are fins designed to radiate heat from the water. This gimmick didn't last long. Too much trouble for too little benefit, if any. The date of this picture is determined by the holes in Griffith's very big straw hat, which he wore briefly during the filming of *The Clansman*."

14

left] A careful reconstruction of Ford's Theater, ready for
Lincoln's assassination in *The Birth of a Nation*. The figure is
that of Griffith in one of his famous hats. The set has been built
open to the sky—a tribute to the Californian sunshine. The
Hollywood hills can just be glimpsed over the top of the set,
which was put up at the Griffith studio on Sunset Boulevard.
Above, the moment after the assassination. Lincoln has been
mortally wounded (a mirror reflects the sun on to him, like a
spotlight), and Booth has uttered "*Sic semper tyrannis!*" and
fled, interrupting the performance of *Our American Cousin*
for ever.

CHAPTER EIGHT

Expanding Empire

The Production of Intolerance

IF Griffith was driven to greater heights by the response to *The Birth of a Nation*, so the industry gained greater confidence. Feature pictures appeared on a more sophisticated range of subjects, even though the one- and two-reelers persisted. In the excitement over Griffith's picture, one tends to forget that the first American super-picture, Selig's eight-reel production of *The Spoilers*, directed by Colin Campbell, had appeared in 1914. But while *The Spoilers* contained impressive episodes—miners struggling with strike-breakers, a massive mine explosion, and the celebrated fight between William Farnum and Thomas Santschi,—and while it was extremely successful, it was not in the same exalted league as Griffith's picture. Campbell tried to outdo *The Birth* in 1916 with another Civil War epic, *The Crisis*, but it failed to attract the popularity of either *The Spoilers* or *The Birth*. Nevertheless, these surges of energy invigorated the industry.

Adolph Zukor, in the ascendant with his Famous Players pictures, was also chastising himself for not having made *The Birth*. He could have done it, for he once owned the property. He told me, when I interviewed him in 1964, that he regarded the sale of *The Clansman* as his greatest mistake. Zukor, a product of the Trust era, having had his own problems with the Patents Company, was rapidly becoming a kind of Trust of his own, absorbing companies and seizing control of the most important stars. To rival Zukor, if not to outdo him, was the ambition of Harry Aitken, who had left Mutual and was busily laying the foundations for an empire. With Griffith as the apex, he formed the Triangle Corporation, with Thomas Ince and Mack Sennett. The idea was that Griffith and Ince would provide dramatic pictures and Sennett the comedy element for programmes of outstanding merit, to be launched in legitimate theatres and distributed at inflated prices. He engaged Broadway stars just as Zukor had—DeWolf Hopper, William Collier Sr, Raymond Hitchcock, Sir Herbert Beerbohm Tree, Constance Collier—and brought them to California in the summer season at huge salaries.

Griffith, with his veneration of the theatre, and his own failure as actor and playwright, must have found the presence in his studio of such luminaries hard to believe. Apparently, they were somewhat bewildered, too.

"Sir Herbert Beerbohm Tree was a complete novice, as far as films were concerned," said Anita Loos. "It was rumoured round the lot that when he first saw the camera, he said 'I can't act in front of that black box. Take it away.' He was making *Macbeth* and the director, John Emerson, couldn't get him to cut down on his speeches. Sir Herbert insisted on spouting every word of *Macbeth* into the camera, which was a terrible waste of film. The cameraman would pull the crank out and let Sir Herbert carry on and on and on, until the director gave him a signal that they were going to film the

action. Sir Herbert never found out that he was spouting *Macbeth* into an empty camera."

It may seem baffling today that anyone considered Shakespeare an appropriate subject for the silent film. Yet such was the volume of Shakespearian adaptations before the coming of sound that an American professor has written an entire book on the subject. *Macbeth* no longer exists, but from all accounts it was a good film; "Lovers of Shakespeare," said *Motion Picture Magazine*, "will find much in the photo-spectacle that the spoken tragedy must miss."

"The point was," said Anita Loos, "that D. W. Griffith had great ambitions for the movies, and he was always trying to better them. It hurt him terribly that they were looked down on as a rowdy entertainment. I think that's what prompted him to do *Macbeth*; he said, 'We're going to do Shakespeare on film,' and it was taking a long step, because Shakespeare without Shakespearian dialogue was a little bit hazardous. I know that in the credits there was a line which said, 'By William Shakespeare. Titles by Anita Loos'."

Before *The Clansman* was premièred, Griffith had made a small-scale feature with Mae Marsh and Bobby Harron called *The Mother and the Law*. Very much in the style of such Biographs as *The Musketeers of Pig Alley*, but more fluid and expressive, it was a social picture about the fortunes of two young people, who are driven from their homes by a strike and struggle for survival in the slums. The girl's baby is seized by reformers; the boy is sentenced to death for a murder he didn't commit. Griffith included a savage sequence of militiamen firing with machine-guns upon strikers, and killing the boy's father. Such a sequence was a hangover from the working-class pictures of the Nickelodeon days; Griffith might have balked at the idea of impugning so American an institution in the patriotic climate of a year or so later. But at the time no one could argue that it libelled the authorities; strikers were constantly being fired upon, by troops or by detectives. It was one of the hazards of industrial disputes. Griffith based the scene on the Ludlow Massacre and the strike at Bayonne, N.J. He took immense pleasure in showing the Reform Movement in operation, and while he didn't go quite as far as *Traffic in Souls*, which had a Reformer heading the white slave traffic, he did show them destroying the lives of a mother and child by tearing them apart. Griffith followed the Dickensian tradition of attacking a social evil rashly rather than rationally. (He made reformers clamour for the censorship of his film; when he reissued it in 1919, he was obliged to show good reformers at work—and a title explains that the troops shooting the strikers were using blanks.)

When the film was finished, it was a modest programme picture. Hardly the sort of thing with which to follow *The Birth of a Nation*. Griffith might still have released it, with a few adjustments, had he not seen the latest Italian extravaganza, *Cabiria*.

To have made a film hailed as the world's greatest masterpiece must have been exhilarating; but then to see a film like *Cabiria* must have been immeasurably depressing. Not that it exceeded the standard of *The Birth* in terms of story, but in terms of physical production and technical dexterity, it made *The Birth* look primeval.

Exactly when Griffith saw it is impossible to surmise. Begun in 1912, it reached America in May of 1914. Karl Brown gives the impression he saw it as soon as he could. "The reviews of *Cabiria* had such an effect on Griffith that he and key members of his staff took the next train to San Francisco to see it." Brown, who was not a key member, waited until it reached Clune's Auditorium. "It was impressive, particularly the great shot of the god Moloch; children were placed on his protruding tongue, and a gush of smoke came out of the mouth. It was really a wonderful picture. It lacked only one element that I can pin-point. It had no story."

Cabiria's plot was of little account. It was visually so staggering that the lack of story-line mattered little until the last reel, when the plot had to be resolved. Probably no silent film, and precious few sound films, have contained imagery of such sustained power and confidence. Obsessed by the third dimension, director Giovanni Pastrone (under the pseudonym Piero Fosco) created shots of remarkable depth, separating the planes with a constantly-moving camera. Griffith must have watched the film with an envy next to despair. How could anyone outdo such magnificence? Griffith *did* outdo it, but his recklessness proved financially disastrous.

The Mother and the Law was shelved, and, as Karl Brown remembers, Griffith began a totally different film, also entitled *The Mother and the Law*—a French story, with *Count of Monte Cristo* swordplay. It was followed by another, totally different story, a Biblical play this time, also called *The Mother and the Law*. The most complicated and challenging film, however, also called *The Mother and the Law*, was set in Babylon, and required the walls of Babylon to be built, full size, on a vacant lot across the street from the Sunset Boulevard studio. Here Griffith set about extinguishing the competition of the Italians, little realising that World War One was doing it for him.

Karl Brown said: "We had just been touring San Quentin, for *The Mother and the Law*, and on the way home, the car stopped at a rise overlooking the Pan-Pacific Exposition ground in San Francisco. The Tower of Jewels was a magnificent sight. It was covered with faceted mock jewels that were turned in the wind, like Chinese wind bells, so the entire structure was alive with glitter. Griffith looked at it in fascination. In *Judith* he had wanted Oriental grandeur, but was unable to get it because he was held down by the penny-pinching Biograph people, who didn't want him to make big pictures anyway. Now he could do it. He had the money that was cascading in from *The Birth of a Nation*. Here below him were the men who had erected this Tower of Jewels. All he had to do was put the workmen together with his dreams, and he had it."

Later, Griffith sent his assistant Joseph Henabery to persuade the workmen to join the company. By this time the Exposition was over, and the people who had built it had left. But Henabery rounded up three of the craftsmen who had worked on the intricate Italian section. Griffith's associates have steadfastly insisted there was no art director; Griffith showed pictures to his boss carpenter, Frank 'Huck' Wortman, and the sets were built accordingly. But Karl Brown remembered Walter L. Hall, an English theatrical designer, who translated Griffith's vision into reality.

Once Babylon towered over Sunset Boulevard, Griffith had to work out how to shoot it. A tall camera tower was an obvious answer, but Griffith had been impressed by those subtle camera movements in *Cabiria*. Could he make the camera move from that height? A balloon was tried, but it made Bitzer sick and was not a stable camera platform. Griffith asked Allan Dwan, an engineer albeit an electrical one, and he suggested a mobile tower with an elevator. It was constructed to move on mining rails. No photograph of this monster is known to exist but the scenes that it filmed are so full of mystery and magic that perhaps it's as well to preserve that mystery. The eye of the audience is guided softly out of the clouds above Babylon and down to examine the Bacchanalian feast below.

"At a certain season of the year," said Karl Brown, "Southern California is visited by a windstorm, a Santa Ana. This wind, blowing out of a cloudless sky, comes in off the San Fernando Valley, which at that time was raw desert. Clouds of dust come over the mountains and through the valley, and a strong wind which would reach forty or fifty knots, so much so that it was hard to walk against. We had put up the walls of Babylon which were about 150 feet long and 90 feet high—that's a considerable area to expose to a wind as any man knows who's used to square-rigged vessels. When the Santa Ana hit that tremendous expanse, the walls were just moving in and out. We thought we'd lost the entire set, but Huck Wortman, our master builder, said 'Well, it ain't no use looking at her, let's get some line on her.' So we did. The boys went aloft on that swinging structure and fastened hawsers, which were made fast and covered with what they called dead men. Those dead men saved our lives, because the hawsers held, the wind subsided and we went to work."

If *The Birth* was an extended Biograph, the new picture broke new ground. Of course, the favourite Griffith elements were there. Constance Talmadge played a Mary Pickford role, and the standard Biograph situation—a family trapped in a hut as marauders batter down the door—was enlarged to show the population of Babylon withstanding the Persian invader. But having started with the modest story of *The Mother and the Law*, Griffith extended the subject into three flashbacks, of increasingly grander scale. They could not be used to consolidate points in the original story without overbalancing it. Having worked without a script, Griffith had no precise plans as to how to integrate the new elements; he just kept shooting. When he ran into financial difficulties with Aitken, who was having problems with Thomas Ince's epic *Civilization* over at Inceville, he invested his own money and encouraged Lillian Gish, Mae Marsh and others to do the same. With the example of *The Birth*, they needed no persuasion.

The first roughcut of the new film ran to eight hours; Griffith was told by exhibitors that a film of even half that length was too long. Under the title *Intolerance*, Griffith eventually produced a version of three hours, fifteen minutes. The editing was one of Griffith's most heroic endeavours. In his efforts to retain all four stories, he devised a method of cross-cutting between each of them which was bold, dynamic and more of an innovation than anything he had claimed in his advertisement. The new technique, while it baffled audiences, exhilarated film makers, who duplicated and expanded it for the next fifty years.

"After *Intolerance* was finished," said Anita Loos, "and D.W. was editing it, he sent for me one day and said, 'I'm going to let you write the titles.' So I sat with Griffith in the projection room, and I think I was the first one to see it, because Griffith worked in the greatest secrecy and nobody acting in *Intolerance* knew what it was about. They were completely bewildered by what D.W. was doing. When he asked me in to see it, I looked at it with awe because it had been such a mystery. I thought it was awful. I couldn't see. I wasn't intelligent enough to see the broad vision of this man. His scrambling of the time elements, which had never been heard of before, was completely bewildering to the audience. It was to me. But I pulled myself together and wrote the titles. Like so many terribly important things in life, when they occur, you don't realise them. I never recognised what an historic moment I was living through, watching that film."

Audiences today, who do not expect to work for their entertainment, find *Intolerance* as difficult as those of 1916. In Mexico, the film was 'arranged' and the four themes separated. The intercutting was never popular outside film circles. As a reviewer put it; "One was fearful lest Belshazzar be run over by an automobile." For those who liked to identify with characters, and become lost in a story, *Intolerance* was irritating; it was plagued by a kind of cinematic tic, which whipped one scene away before anyone had time to digest it, and startled you with another. You found yourself admiring the sets instead of feeling for the characters. The violence was upsetting, too; I remember the shock of seeing the film myself for the first time when I was thirteen. Some mischievous friend had assured me that an extra was accidentally beheaded during the making of the film and, when I saw Elmo Lincoln lop the head off a Persian, I was so shaken I couldn't sleep for a week.

Yet one must acknowledge that at first, audiences in America supported the picture. Reviewers praised it as "better than *The Birth*" and "the world's greatest motion picture", and the trade press considered it, "Stupendous, tremendous, revolutionary, intense, thrilling, and you can throw away the old typewriter and give up with the dictionary because you can't find adjectives enough." (*Film Daily*). For the first few weeks, the picture did outstanding business at first-run theatres, but business fell off after four months. Four months was an amazing run when most pictures ran for a week, but *Intolerance* was not most pictures. Its negative cost, according to a Price-Waterhouse audit was $485,000—the price of forty ordinary films. With his respect for the theatre, Griffith insisted on roadshowing *Intolerance*, accompanying the film with huge orchestras. The result was that the roadshow expenses ate up the profit. "It did not fail as compared with the grosses of other pictures. It failed only because it cost much more than even an enormously successful picture would have brought in," said Karl Brown.

The failure of *Intolerance* was ultimately ensured by America's move towards war.

"That was something which could not be foreseen," said Karl Brown. "There is a problem faced by all who make pictures, publish books, or do anything in which a time element is involved. You must guess what will be the popular rage twelve, fourteen, eighteen months from now. In Griffith's case, when he started 'Intolerance' he wanted to sting home the idea that it was man's inhumanity to man that made thousands weep, as Pope said. And he did so in the most uncompromising terms; it is hatred and intolerance that makes all the misery in the world. What he did not realise was that in the 18 months that he was making that picture, America, from being a pacifist nation whose popular song was 'I didn't raise my boy to be a soldier, to kill some other mother's darling boy', had turned to Hate the Hun. Meanwhile, Griffith was preaching peace on earth and goodwill toward men. How could such a sermon do anything but fail in a nation that was rabid for war?"

Shakespeare on silent film suggests a pointless exercise—but it was
one way to attract the theatre people to the movies, thus providing
inestimable prestige. Sir Herbert Beerbohm Tree (left) and
Constance Collier (centre) played the leads in *Macbeth* (1916) under
the direction of John Emerson. D. W. Griffith (right) pays a visit to
the set.

left] When production began on *Cabiria*, in 1912, the future of the Italian industry seemed assured. The Americans were still at a primitive stage, with hardly a feature film to their credit. By 1914, when *Cabiria* was released, the entire situation had changed. The Americans had made enormous strides. Griffith had made his own 'Italian' epic, *Judith of Bethulia*, and was planning *The Birth of a Nation*. Nevertheless, the visual standard of *Cabiria* was so far ahead of anything the Americans could produce that the Italians feared no competition. What they didn't foresee was World War One, which left their industry crippled. *Cabiria* led directly to the Babylonian sequences of *Intolerance*, and the *motif* of the elephant, with its trunk aloft, found its way to Griffith's massive set.

right] The celluloid Babylon was achieved without the benefit of art director, according to many of those who worked on *Intolerance*. It was Karl Brown, in his book *Adventures with D. W. Griffith*, who introduced the long-forgotten Walter Hall; an English stage designer, Hall translated Griffith's vision on to paper. This is one of his drawings.

below] This picture has appeared in so many film histories, that I repeat it here only for reference, to provide a context for the pictures which accompany it.

left] The Babylon set for *Intolerance* in the course of construction, on a site near the intersection of Sunset and Hollywood Boulevards. The elephants on the right of the big set have been placed in position, and some of the massive columns have gone up.

(The shadow in the foreground is cast by a typical Hollywood street sign, with a bell denoting the route of El Camino Real— the royal highway of old Spanish California.)

above] The back of the famous set, with the elephants just visible (on both sides of the arch). The picture has been completed, and the title changed from *The Mother and the Law* to *Intolerance*. The fire department regarded the sets as a fire hazard and insisted they be torn down. But when Griffith ran into difficulties with Triangle, he used the sets as headquarters for *Hearts of the World* (see page 88), after which Babylon finally crumbled.

77

If our view of modern history is based on photographs, newsreels and eye-witness accounts, our idea of ancient history is largely based on films like *Intolerance*. Who could question Griffith's view of Babylon? He based his ideas on paintings, whose artists certainly took pains with their research, but who also employed liberal artistic licence—as demonstrated in the engraving by Edwin Long Pinx of a Marriage Market in Babylon. Griffith has separated the auctioneer and customers more clearly from the slaves; in other respects, the similarities are striking. Madame Sul Te-Wan (grandmother of Dorothy Dandridge, black star of a later age) holds the slave's garments.

CHAPTER NINE

Intolerance Flourishes

World War One

IF World War One eroded the fortunes of those who lived in Europe, it created fortunes for those who ran the American film industry.

"World War One was the reason for Hollywood," said Anita Loos. "At the time war broke out, movies had gained a very substantial place in Europe. They were being made in France, and in Italy they were particularly good, and there was no need for Hollywood. But the war broke out and that changed the whole scene. It was impossible to work with the economics of war surrounding these studios. So I really credit Hollywood on World War One."

American films had been gaining on their European rivals in the years immediately before the war but France, Italy and Sweden held their dominance. American trade papers, apart from being astonished by the Italian imports, also began to notice the German cinema. Theatre producer–owner Al Woods had moved into Berlin and acquired a number of motion picture theatres. And when *Red Powder* was imported in 1913, reviewers said, "The Germans are beginning to be heard from."

The outbreak of the war was greeted with ill-concealed glee among American manufacturers, who scrambled for any piece of film with a war slant. The generally accepted opinion that the whole thing would be over by Christmas restrained their hand as far as production of war films went; President Wilson also pleaded for the neutrality shown by the United States to be shown, too, in motion picture theatres. On the whole, Americans obeyed. War was the kind of old-world activity from which many of them had fled, but a a few ardent nationalists wrecked theatres showing films they disliked. Nationals of those countries involved in the war were called to the colours, and fortunately for film history, men like Erich von Stroheim and Maurice Tourneur failed to obey.

Film makers were galvanised by the sinking of the *Lusitania* in 1915. Germany instantly became the enemy, for Americans had been among the victims, and the spectre of submarine warfare loomed over American foreign policy. J. Stuart Blackton, one of the heads of the Vitagraph Corporation, climbed aboard the Preparedness bandwagon and produced an epic called *Battle Cry of Peace* to show what might happen if the United States was invaded. Since America was neutral, Blackton didn't want to cause an international incident by naming the 'enemy', but the costume and behaviour left audiences in no doubt. The picture was immensely successful and guaranteed a whole series of nightmare pictures in which foreign armies swept across American soil. William Randolph Hearst, who was considered pro-German, attempted to divert fears from the Hun to an enemy closer to home: the Mexican. Hearst had lost vast ranches in Mexico as a result of the revolution, and in a serial called *Patria*, he spread his bigotry generously, involving both the Japanese and the Mexicans in an invasion of America.

Almost every American picture about the war was pro-Ally, not for any nationalistic reason—the manufacturers, with names like Selig, Laemmle, Zukor, Baumann, mostly hailed from Central Europe—but because they wanted their films distributed through London. The nerve centre of the Empire, London was the largest film clearing house in the world. Some American films reached Germany, but precious few; the Allied naval blockade ensured that.

The slogans on the wall from the November 1916 election—"Our President kept us out of the war"—formed a reproachful background to the parades and demonstrations when the United States declared war. Americans were stunned by this volte-face, and the huge German population exceedingly unhappy. Mobilisation and a sudden rise in the cost of living to pay for the war caused a slump in the motion picture business. Some theatres closed, and studios were also affected; the number of films produced in 1917 fell dramatically.

But Hollywood expressed enthusiasm for the war effort. "Everyone was wildly patriotic," said Jesse Lasky, Jr. "Mrs DeMille and Mrs Fairbanks and all the ladies were rolling bandages and wearing nurses' costumes around Hollywood, looking for wounded. Every Thursday night, the studio contingent formed the Lasky Home Guard, with prop rifles and uniforms from the wardrobe department. The whole family of the studio used to go out in uniform and march behind the band down Hollywood Boulevard, and thus we knew we were safe from the Germans. Thursday night was always the greatest night of my life, because it was a chance to play soldier."

Cecil B. DeMille, as director general of the Famous Players–Lasky studios, was placed in charge.

"Cecil was a captain, naturally," said Agnes de Mille, his niece. "He had no right to be, but he just was. He had gone to military school as a young man, so he knew something, and he read up on his manuals. They drilled very faithfully and then they had a final drill out at the Lasky ranch and some of the men went to France. Mary Pickford presented them with their colours, and I remember Mrs Pickford saying she'd had it all made out of silk, the finest silk, and all the stars were hand embroidered. Mary had a special couturier's outfit of patriotic grey, with a little veil down the back. She looked splendid. When he said goodbye to the boys, Cecil's voice broke and he was really overcome with it. Mary, however, like a little soldier, stood up and sent them to their death very valiantly. The grisly part is that some did go to their death."

The war effort could not survive without a constant replenishment of funds, and the government created a scheme called the Liberty Loan. Such enormous sums were needed that the government enlisted the aid of the leading film stars. Douglas

Fairbanks, Mary Pickford and Charlie Chaplin could summon a larger crowd than any politician, and could charm dollars out of the wallets of people who couldn't even hear them. All the prominent stars were involved in war work of one kind or another. For the Treasury department Chaplin, Fairbanks and Pickford made Liberty Bond shorts which were distributed free to the theatres; stars of less spell-binding magnitude toured hospitals and cantonments on morale-boosting missions.

The government recognised the value of stars as crowd-pullers, yet they distrusted the industry as a whole. Factual films about the war were given not to the film distributors for distribution, but to the Red Cross. Such films could not be photographed by motion picture people, but by the US Army. The Signal Corps set up a unit to film and photograph the whole gigantic operation, and quickly ran into trouble when its soldiers proved inept. Motion picture people were hastily drafted to fill the breach, and a large number of Hollywood cameramen served in the Signal Corps.

The British Government's attitude was no more enlightened than the American; at first it had forbidden cameramen anywhere near the front. But when the value of propaganda films became apparent, it invited D. W. Griffith to make a film for the Allied Cause. The government saw nothing paradoxical about the man responsible for a great pacifist film producing a great war film; nor did Griffith, who revelled in the assignment. He toured the front lines, and had some film taken in France. But he expressed his disappointment with war. 'The dash and thrill of wars of other days' was missing. The rapid movement behind the lines excited him, and he brought back much documentary footage, but the front-line action he created on Salisbury Plain, and on the Lasky Ranch in Hollywood.

Convinced of the commercial magnetism of the war, American producers put into their schedules anti-German films which had enormous impact across the world—far more impact than anything produced by the government. The German High Command acknowledged this, and inaugurated their own government-run film corporation, in a vain attempt to combat them. American films, by this time, were so popular in neutral countries that the Germans found themselves obliged to include a Norma Talmadge or Douglas Fairbanks feature in order to attract enough people to put across their own propaganda message.

The anti-German pictures were a blot on the American cinema; how anyone took such melodramatic nonsense seriously is hard to imagine today. Yet equally absurd films were made about the Germans and Japanese in World War Two. They all followed the same pattern. The Germans were portrayed as arrogant, swaggering and viciously cruel. Erich von Stroheim, a young Austrian immigrant, found his niche for the duration playing odious, aristocratic Prussian officers. In *The Unbeliever*, he tears a small boy's hair out by the roots before despatching the rest of the family by a firing squad. In *Heart of Humanity* he rapes a young nurse and throws a baby out of the window. He had been intended for the role of von Strohm (a name which recurs throughout the silent era for vicious German and Russian officers) in *Hearts of the World*, but Griffith lost confidence at the last

moment and gave the part to George Siegmann; von Stroheim was obliged to play his adjutant.

"I remember when I first met him," said his widow, Valerie von Stroheim, "he said, 'I want you to see a picture that I worked in.' We went to a little theatre out on North Broadway, and I see him on the screen, and he's shooting an apple off an old lady's head. Then he shoots her. And so I said, 'We'd better get out of the theatre before the lights are turned on.'"

Von Stroheim was spat at in the street, and pelted with bread rolls when he visited restaurants. "The trouble was," said Mrs von Stroheim, "they used to hit me."

The Hun-hating reached its apotheosis with a film allegedly based on the personal experiences of the US Ambassador to Germany. "Fact, not fiction!" declared the subtitles of *My Four Years in Germany* (1918). The film showed the condition of interned civilians, who were subjected to starvation and disease, and it caused anguish for their relatives, who assumed that scenes actually shot in New Jersey were newsreels. Few of the atrocities shown in the film were committed by the German armies in World War One; they were not, for instance, guilty of the mass execution of civilians.

Blanche Sweet was at work on *The Unpardonable Sin* late in 1918; "When we received this letter," she said, "saying 'cut down on the German atrocities' we knew the war was over."

"When you were making those atrocity pictures," I asked her, "did you know that you were exaggerating?"

"We didn't exaggerate the atrocities," she replied. "They were there. They were in the newspapers. Or are you saying newspapers exaggerated them? I don't know—who are you going to go by? Who's going to tell you what's exaggerated and what isn't? What other way have you?"

The American film industry had been aroused to such a pitch that a letter from Washington was not enough to turn it off. The movies had clearly shown the effectiveness with which they could exploit a nation's latent hatred, and the box office had shown its profitability. Now came the armistice, and President Wilson's call for a Peace with Honour. From the Hollywood and New York studios came films calling for the execution of German militarists, and the hanging of the Kaiser in Times Square. But the public were no longer interested. The war fever subsided as rapidly as it had grown, and the film industry was caught unprepared, with millions of dollars' worth of war films that the public didn't want to see. Some of them were scrapped, some were reshot and some simply withered in half-empty theatres. The revulsion whipped up by the movies and the propaganda machine against the Germans spread to anything connected with the war. There was no precedent for this; after the Civil War, audiences remained passionate about war plays. Now it was necessary to place signs outside theatres assuring the public; 'This is not a war film'.

The spread of Bolshevism in Europe, the German Spartacist uprising and the brief reign of socialism in Hungary, enabled the movies to arouse the old fears, to depict the old villainy; all they had to do was change the uniforms. 1919 was the year of the Red Terror in America; films like *The German Curse in Russia* established the culpability of Germany in shattering the Russian economy and leaving it open to revolution. No attempt was made to tell the facts about Communism; the old fears of autocracy, armed might, infiltration and invasion were whipped up in films like *Dangerous Hours* (1919), produced by Thomas Ince who, only four years earlier, had made a pacifist epic called *Civilization*. While freedom had been won in Europe, it began to fade from America; suspected socialists, Bolsheviks and anarchists were rounded up and, in at least one case, paraded in chains through a town as surrogate German prisoners. Some of the victims were lynched; many were deported to the Soviet Union, where famine and starvation awaited men whose only crime, in many cases, was to have suspicious neighbours.

The last wave of immigration also brought about deep resentment. Once the Irish had been the focus of violence and repression, now it was the turn of the Italians. Fear of the Mafia had brought attacks on innocent Italian families, and among those deported to Russia were many with Italian names. Two anarchists of a pacifist persuasion, Sacco and Vanzetti, were arrested for murder and held for several years in American jails before being executed amidst a tumult of international protest long after the Red Scare had been forgotten. The Mafia and Communism grew to become the twin spectres of America's nightmare, and these early attempts to pluck them out by the roots proved more harmful than helpful.

With war films dead at the box office, and those of Italian appearance discouraged by casting directors, the box office sensation of 1921 surprised Hollywood. Rex Ingram's *The Four Horsemen of the Apocalypse* was almost as impressive a saga of a family's struggles with war as *The Birth of a Nation* had been. Its star was a young Italian, Rudolph Valentino. While the mood of the film veered towards pacifism, with a mystical element which suited the nation's idealism, it opened all the old sores about German brutality. It also sparked off a new argument; who had won the war? The French were maddened by the emphasis on the Americans; the British by the fact that they were virtually left out; the Germans by the parody of their officers.

What was beyond doubt was that Hollywood stood supreme. As a direct result of the war, London had lost its dominant position as the film clearing house for the world to New York. The picture business in America faced the problems the other industries faced: inflation, the flu epidemic and the post-war slump. Theatres across the country closed as the flu epidemic increased its grip, and some studios stopped production. But as the disease lifted, so the industry began to expand. Foreign competition had been virtually wiped out, Eastern studios had fled to California to avoid the fuel shortages, and Hollywood at last became the centre of the film-producing nations of the world.

Ballyhoo for the Fourth Liberty Loan drive Oct 2, 1918. The aggressive men in the foreground are pursuing the dollars of a vast crowd behind the camera. The centrepiece is 'Victory', a mock-up of a tank —real tanks were too precious to spare for such sideshows as this. (In any case, no American tanks reached the front line before the armistice.) Sitting on the tank, signing autographs, is Bessie Love, the enchanting star discovered by D. W. Griffith, who is still acting in pictures today. The number of bonds sold at the meeting by the time the photo was taken can just be discerned behind the man with the megaphone.

The Liberty Bond drives involved many motion picture stars, but those who attracted the largest crowds were Douglas Fairbanks, Charlie Chaplin and Mary Pickford. (They were later brought together in United Artists as a direct result of their war work.) Here, Fairbanks and Chaplin entertain a crowd from the Sub-Treasury steps, Wall Street, New York City during the Third Liberty Bond drive. Only a minority of the crowd could ever hope to hear them—there was no public address system in those days beyond a simple megaphone—but lack of words had not held them back on the screen. Nor did it worry them on the Bond drives. Launching into pantomime, they delighted their audience into parting with hard-earned dollars—something the government soon realised that no politician could ever do.

D. W. Griffith was the only American film director permitted to visit the front lines, and he was tremendously proud of the fact. Unhappily, the battles he had hoped to photograph were fought by men who seldom saw their enemy, and they lacked the dash and colour his audiences—and he—expected. So he recreated them on Salisbury Plain and in California. Nevertheless, some extraordinary film survives in the Imperial War Museum, London, showing Griffith touring the trenches.

left] The situation requires no explanation; even after sixty years, the threat of torture and rape by the unspeakable Hun, and the cool courage of the noble lady, are all too familiar. A scene from *The Unpardonable Sin* with Bull Montana and Blanche Sweet. The picture was in production when the armistice was signed— it was therefore advertised with a blatant disregard for the truth as 'NOT a war picture'.

A most remarkable example of detective work; this original still from *Hearts of the World* (left) had been crudely covered with paint to illustrate an article about Griffith at the front in a 1918 issue of *Photoplay*. When we acquired it for the series, from John Kobal, we asked our graphics designer, Barry O'Riordan, if he could restore it by removing the paint—but to photograph it first in case of problems. He said it was like restoring a Rembrandt, for as he gradually washed the paint away, a very familiar face emerged—that of Erich von Stroheim. While von Stroheim appeared in *Hearts of the World*, in a minor role, there has long been controversy over his role as military adviser. But here is proof positive; von Stroheim adjusting the *képi* of a French soldier. Also revealed is George Siegmann, Griffith's assistant, who played the German officer, a role originally intended for von Stroheim.

Billy Bitzer at camera, Josephine Crowell (centre) and Griffith in another of his famous hats. The background is the *Intolerance* set, where Griffith worked when he lost control of his old studio on Sunset Boulevard.

These scenes symbolise the change in attitude from the propaganda films—like *The Little American* (1917) (*left*), with Mary Pickford—with their emphasis on Huns, humiliation and hatred, to postwar escapist films—like *The Affairs of Anatol* (1921), with Wallace Reid—with their emphasis on fun, fashion and frivolity. Both were directed by Cecil B. DeMille.

CHAPTER TEN

Why Hollywood?

Sun, Space and Somnolence

WHILE it is hard to imagine American films without Hollywood, the industry flourished for years without it. Films were produced all over the United States, but the industry's centre was the nation's financial core, New York. Winters in New York were severe, however, and the more prosperous companies would move *en masse* to Jacksonville, Florida—a mere twenty-seven hour train journey from the metropolis.

For locations, the New York film makers made full use of the East Side ghettoes, the parks and the mansions. The countryside was within easy reach—the 42nd St or 125th St ferries crossed the Hudson River to New Jersey, where there were dense woods, soaring palisades and enough open space to pass for the West. A convenient saloon at Fort Lee, Rambo's, had a front that could double for a western bar and a rear that could serve as a darkroom. With New Jersey offering cheaper real estate than New York, film manufacturers established studios in Fort Lee until the place became a film factory town.

The constant fear of Patents Company detectives emptied the town of all but the most trenchant independents, and the example of California-made films—so clear and sharp and with such wonderful backgrounds—was highly tempting to the others. The Los Angeles Chamber of Commerce guaranteed sunshine for 350 days of the year, and Selig, a Chicago-based company, sent a crew to see if it was true. They produced a few films in Los Angeles before trying Colorado—and announcing their preference for Los Angeles. Essanay also travelled the West, but they discarded Los Angeles because of antagonism from the police, and settled at Niles Canyon, near Oakland, in Northern California. The American Film Company began production at Lakeside, California, then moved to La Mesa, and finally built a substantial studio at Santa Barbara. The Bison Company had a ranch at Santa Monica, and the Biograph had a makeshift studio next to the streetcar barns at Pico and Georgia Street, Los Angeles. Here, D. W. Griffith would arrive with his players every New Year's Day to winter in the sunshine. From such studios, the picture people would occasionally travel out to the little town of Hollywood, which provided an ideal small-town atmosphere, whose attributes seemed to be sun, space and somnolence.

Hollywood was famous for its fruit—the Cahuenga Valley in which it was situated was known as the Frostless Belt. Orange and lemon groves stretched across the valley, and the yield was so impressive that it attracted tourists. Hollywood's founding father was a real estate practitioner, Harvey Henderson Wilcox, whose wife had changed the name of their Cahuenga Valley–Wilcox Ranch to the more euphonious Hollywood. Wilcox's passion was real estate, and he made a map of what the area around Hollywood Ranch might look like were it subdivided. No sooner was the map distributed to real estate agents than Wilcox's imaginings became reality. Tourists, already impressed by the fruit yield, frequently fell in love with the place, acquired lots and helped to push the real estate prices up over a hundred per cent in three months.

Prestige was the first requirement of the little town, once it had acquired the nucleus of a population. Advertisements boosting the Frostless Belt and the stupendous yields were disseminated across the country, but soon such advertising was unnecessary, for Hollywood acquired one of the most prized showplaces in Southern California. Curiously enough, it was also Hollywood's first studio. Paul de Longpré, a French painter of flowers, had settled in Los Angeles because flowers in New York were too expensive and not varied enough. Harvey Wilcox's widow offered him a site on Hollywood Boulevard if he would establish his studio there. He went one better; in 1902 he acquired the whole corner lot in return for three paintings, and built a palatial home surrounded by superbly cultivated grounds which attracted thousands of tourists a year. He was a hospitable man—his wife was expert at French cuisine—and he made newspaper men especially welcome. The result was that the name of Hollywood and of de Longpré soon became nationally celebrated. Long before the arrival of the motion picture people, the History of Hollywood could claim; "Never was free column publicity so lavishly bestowed on a single community."

1911 was a significant year for Hollywood, and the end to all hopes of preserving its exclusive atmosphere. Paul de Longpré died, and an era faded, but thanks to the puritanical elders of the town, a new one was preordained. The City Fathers had banned everything they could think of that might lower the tone, such as the establishment of gasworks or slaughterhouses, but they overlooked the moving picture people. From their occasional appearance in the town, the City Fathers assumed their occupation was a transient one, like travelling road companies. In any case, they were concerned with far more immediate issues such as alcohol. Wilcox had been a prohibitionist and many of the other residents, mostly mid-westerners, supported his stand.

On Sunset Boulevard was a roadhouse managed by a French family, the Blondeaus. Louis Blondeau had bought the place from Wilcox, obeying his strictures against operating a saloon until Wilcox's death, when the place began to boom. To his chagrin, Hollywood passed an ordinance prohibiting the sale of liquor, and the Blondeau roadhouse suffered from drought.

It was therefore no surprise when Mrs Blondeau leased it to some moving picture people—representatives of the Centaur Film Company, Bayonne, New Jersey, who were searching for a permanent Californian base. Their western operation was named Nestor, and the Nestor studio became the first in Hollywood.

The New York Motion Picture Company had opened a studio in

Edendale in 1909, and Mack Sennett occupied it in 1912. Vitagraph opened a western branch in Santa Monica in 1911. A group of studios—the Universal, Eclair and Lasky—opened up around Sunset Boulevard in Hollywood itself, and the rapid proliferation of film factories within the town caused the Board of Trade to sponsor a zoning ordinance. Hollywood was thus spared the fate of becoming the true centre of film production, but it was still the most attractive of all the suburbs around Los Angeles, and it boasted a fine hotel, the Hollywood Hotel. For this reason, the picture people gravitated to Hollywood, rented rooms at the hotel and began to buy homes in the town.

The variety of scenery in Southern California was unmatched anywhere in the world, and the California-made pictures soon carried their locations proudly on their posters. The Cahuenga Valley seemed a Garden of Eden to the new arrivals from the East.

Said Agnes de Mille; "The sage brush and the rain . . . the eucalyptus in the rain . . . you see, the spring was such a marvellous thing there. The English spring which I knew is a miracle. But in Hollywood you got through the summer and autumn—the summer was just brown bare, burnt brown like the desert, and then the autumn became rather dangerous for fires. And then came the rains. They were hard-driving, down-pouring, almost tropical rains, and they'd be of two or three days duration, and then we'd have floods. All of the arroyos flooded, a great many streets gave way and people were drowned. It became part of the goings on.

"When the rains came, within two weeks what had been brown was suddenly all green, and the grass there is so strong, with a virility somehow that is just exciting. And in the grass would be tangled the lupins, the poppies, the brodiaea, all of them exquisite, and all of them just blooming wild and in the gutter. You gathered them by the armful.

"The streets ran right into the foothills, and the foothills went straight up into sage brush, and you were in the wild, wild hills. Sage brush, and rattlesnakes, and coyotes and the little wild deer that came down every night. I was forbidden to go up to the end of the street alone, because you were right among the rattlesnakes; it was a very sane prohibition, I think.

"Franklin Avenue was then just a street, absolutely arced, pouring with pepper branches and Vine Street had palm trees and pepper trees lining it—those were very beautiful, graceful trees. They've all been cut down since. It's a pity."

The pepper trees were cut down because their berries had the unfortunate habit of falling on automobile hoods and corroding them. The eucalyptus trees were imported from Australia, and while some palms were indigenous to California, Hollywood imported others from Hawaii.

Sunset Boulevard snaked through the hills, following an old cattle trail, and petered out long before the coast. For some of its length, a bridle path ran down the centre, for the horse was the most sensible method of transport in Hollywood. Few of the roads were paved, and some of the studios provided hitching rails.

"Of course there were automobiles," said Jesse Lasky Jr, "they'd had them for twenty years, but there weren't many. The studio had two or three for general purposes, but we had horses and we rode to school. There was a sign I remember on the back of the street car that said 'Don't shoot rabbits from the rear platform.' I think they were afraid they might hit the policeman—Hollywood had one policeman, and he generally stood at the corner of Hollywood and Vine."

The constancy of the sunshine was a vital economic factor, for manufacturers could depend on making films without lights. But Southern California was popular for another reason; labour costs were half what they were in New York. Los Angeles was well known for being a non-union town, and there were plentiful supplies of Mexican and Oriental workers. Extras were cheap, and sometimes free, local people being willing to act for the fun of it.

The financial offices of the motion picture operations remained in New York, New Jersey or Chicago, separated from their studios by a train journey of four days. This situation improved the profits of Western Union and the Santa Fe and did little to lower the profits of the picture companies, so it was allowed to continue. The financial people needed to be in the East, close to the pulse of the stock market, and they relied on supervisors, studio managers and occasional snap inspections, to keep their studios up to the mark. But the gulf between production and administration led to creeping inefficiency. By the end of the silent era, the producers had reorganised and strengthened the western end of their business, and many had moved permanently to California.

Motion picture people in Hollywood were known by the locals as 'movies'. They lived modestly at first, by show business standards, but their high spirits and free-and-easy manner offended some of the older residents. "The residents were horrified," said Anita Loos, "because they were very modest people, mostly from the middle west, people who were elderly and had gone out to California to sit in the sunshine for their declining years, so when they saw this troupe of scallywags show up they felt the community was being harmed."

"We were beneath them," said Allan Dwan. "If we walked in the streets with our cameras, they hid their girls under the beds and closed the doors and the windows and shied away. We were really tramps in their eyes."

"I knew what racial discrimination was because I was a 'movie'", said Agnes de Mille, "and it was just not permitted for us to know people. You may not believe this, but I met a highly intelligent and charming girl my age, which was nine, and she was asked to come and spend the night at our house, and I can remember my mother on the telephone to her mother saying, 'But my father, who was a very conservative man, said it was so broadening to see how other people lived.' And this woman kept saying, 'But you might go to the movies,' and mother said, 'Yes, we might, but we won't if you don't want us to.' Well, it just doesn't seem possible. We crashed that barrier and finally got the little girl to come home and spend the night with me. And she got home untainted, apparently."

The suspicion was not universal. At Edendale, where William Hornbeck lived and where his mother had sold some land to the New York Motion Picture Company, the residents welcomed the picture business because it provided work for the local community.

"I can remember my uncle going out as a soldier," said Hornbeck, "he was in a Civil War picture, and he was so pleased to put on a uniform and get his dollar—they were getting a dollar a day. I remember it was the first time we had seen paper money; everything on the West Coast was gold or silver. And when he came home with this piece of paper money which the movie people were using he thought it was a fake."

There were no casting organisations in these early days; people gathered at studio gates for work. Allan Dwan remembered: "If our gates were not open they'd rush off to the next little place where they had a gate. And I say 'little places' because they were vacant lots. When we did put up buildings we called studios, they were simply posts stuck up in the air with wires stretched across them and canvas to shield us from the sun. They were called stages. As time advanced, enterprising people came from the East and began to put up buildings around these lots—always leaving the roofs open because otherwise we couldn't work. We had no electric light. They were all open air shots. Sometimes when it was raining, there would be a rush of people to the lot to grab a piece of furniture and get it out of the rain until it had passed, then we'd put it out again, and while the sun was up, shoot a few scenes and then hide the furniture again from the elements. Sometimes it would be raining on one side of the street and we'd make rain shots, and then walk across the street and do sunshine shots."

The thought that fame might touch the most insignificant of mortals eventually gave Hollywood the special aura of a Mecca. Rags-to-riches stories undoubtedly occurred—no more astonishing example of the two extremes could be found than that of Mary Pickford—but most people found the touch of fame highly elusive. Even when chosen by the movies, your part was likely to be insignificant. But if you were looking for fun, that was different.

"On the way to work in the morning," said King Vidor, "I would see a boy selling newspapers on the corner and I'd say, 'He's a good type for the part.' I'd go up to him and say, 'How many papers you got left?' He'd say, 'Fifty, sixty cents.' I'd say, 'Okay, here's the sixty cents. You want to be a movie actor? Leave the papers there and come to work.' We gave him five dollars a day."

"They were great days," said Harvey Parry. "There were no unions, so there was no overtime. You worked Sundays and holidays—no extra pay. But it was a family, a very close-knit group of people. Everybody would help each other. They wouldn't try to hinder you or push you down. Everybody worked. And it was fun, it was real fun."

Because the business was so new, there was a strong sense of optimism and little jealousy and resentment; those spectres of an overcrowded industry came later. There was also a strong communal sense.

"Whenever they finished a picture," said Agnes de Mille, "which would be roughly every week, they wouldn't waste time. They'd paste it together and run it and they asked everybody—all the families, all the children, even neighbours, sometimes—'Come in, come in and see our picture.' Then they'd ask everybody what they thought. I cannot believe it was that simple, but it was, and I think some of that simplicity and some of that fervour and excitement is in the films, and that's why they're valuable and lovely."

This picture sums up the atmosphere of film-making in California in the early days. There is something about the optimism of expression, and the incongruity of costume, that is very appealing. The photograph was taken around 1914; Scott R. Beal, assistant director, and cameraman Roy Overbaugh, are at work for the American Film Company ('Flying A') at Santa Barbara. The camera is the original 1912 edition of the Bell and Howell.

Both men are dressed for the city, and look out of place against the rolling hills. (Before long, they would adopt the distinctive movie uniform of breeches, high boots and khaki shirts.) Their stiff celluloid collars will not be worn much longer, for the picture business helped make them obsolete. Audiences saw so many films from California, with actors wearing soft collars for comfort, that the market for stiff collars dwindled.

Overbaugh wears his cap back to front because the peak prevents him peering through the viewfinder. This became the fashion for cameramen in the silent era.

What the moving picture people found: Hollywood in 1905, before the invasion. We are looking down on Hollywood Boulevard, which runs along the centre. The road on the right is Orange Drive, and the house with the oriental cupola became the home of Conway Tearle. More recently, it passed into the hands of the American Society of Cinematographers, who have carefully preserved it—the only building in the picture to survive. Apartment and office blocks now stretch to the horizon.

The Blondeau roadhouse, leased to moving picture people because of a prohibition against liquor, became the first studio in Hollywood in 1911. It was acquired by the Horsley Brothers, a couple of Englishmen who operated the Centaur Film Company in Bayonne, New Jersey. They called their western branch Nestor. Nestor's studio was on the corner of Sunset Boulevard and Gower Street. The backs of sets can be glimpsed behind the building.

below] 1913; The Selig Company, having just moved in to 3800, Mission Road, in Eastlake Park, have thoughtfully provided a walkway to prevent cast and technicians trampling the corn. Companies can work side by side on this stage, the muslin diffusers softening the harsh rays of the sun.

However nostalgic one might feel about the old studios, one must acknowledge that they despoiled the landscape. Top left is Edendale, not far from Hollywood, in 1905. Alessandro Street runs through the centre of the picture (with trolley car tracks prominent). The corner lot, at centre right, belonged to a family called Hornbeck, who sold an adjoining lot to the New York Motion Picture Company in 1909. Soon, the studio passed to Mack Sennett's Keystone Comedies, and young William Hornbeck was taken on to run errands. (Before long, he was running the editing department, and he developed into one of

the industry's great editors, with such credits as *Giant* and *Place in the Sun*.)

By 1921, (bottom left) Edendale looked like a factory town—which is what it was, for several studios had been established here. The Sennett studios advertise their romantic drama, "the first the Comedy King has yet produced", *Heart Balm* (released as *Crossroads of New York*). The lower picture covers the right-hand portion of the upper photograph. The area is now usually known as Glendale, or Echo Park.

Director King Vidor and his wife, actress Florence Vidor, at their home on Sierra Bonita Avenue, in Hollywood, 1918. The Vidors managed to make film making a family concern for a while; they had their own small studio—Vidor Village—on Santa Monica Boulevard.

When it rained in California, before the advent of closed stages, there was a rush to rescue the furniture and props. The shooting of interiors stopped—and the shooting of exteriors, too, unless someone could dream up a good rain sequence. At the Lasky studio, the DeMille company keeps right on shooting *Romance of the Redwoods* (1917), protected by tarpaulins and umbrellas. The light comes from Klieg lights—theatrical arc lights manufactured by the Kliegl Brothers (current joke: "who knocked the 'l' out of Kliegl?") which can be seen to the left of the group.

left] An early morning call on a chilly glass stage at the Thomas Ince studios in Culver City, 1919. Dorothy Dalton warms her hands over a salamander, while assistant director Bert Siebel runs over her scenes in the script.

Curious onlookers line a Hollywood street to watch the production
of *The Ghost House*, a Lasky Feature Play, 1917. Some of the
more athletic perch on telephone poles. This eager interest was not
emulated by Los Angeles public officials, some of whom were
openly hostile to the expanding industry. Matters had come to a head
in 1915, when two companies announced they were contemplating
moving their studios to a town "with more encouragement and
courtesy". They objected to being refused access to public parks,
and having their work interfered with by petty officials. At a
meeting of the Merchants' and Manufacturers' Association some
startling facts and figures were read out; the film industry, in the
Los Angeles area alone, expended $5 million per year on salaries
and supplies, and employed more than 25,000 people. "Aside from
the financial advantages, Los Angeles derives a tremendous
advertising feature by having our scenic beauties and climatic
advantages depicted in pictures seen by the theater-going public
throughout the United States." The Association deplored the
attitude of the officials—and pledged their co-operation in future.

right] A typical scene in Griffith Park in the 'twenties, as a movie
company packs up, ready to move to another location. The film is
Name the Man (1924) from a story by Hall Caine. The director,
standing right, is the great Victor Seastrom. The cameraman
(hand on tripod), is Charles van Enger.

Visitors to Hollywood, hoping to see wonderful sets, were invariably
disappointed. Few of the studios admitted visitors—only Universal
did so as a matter of policy—and travellers tended to complain that
everything was "so damned unimpressive". However, if you looked
for one, it was unusual not to encounter a company at work in the
streets. Residents were infuriated at the high-handed attitude of the
picture people, taking over entire streets and roping in passers-by,
but visitors found it fascinating. Here a company from the Mack
Sennett studios get ready to shoot a scene for a Ben Turpin
comedy. At centre is Sennett himself.

One reason for the antipathy of local residents towards film people was the frequency with which their calm was shattered. Cowboys would ride over their manicured lawns . . . Keystone Cops' paddy-wagons would skid down their street . . . wild animals would escape from the motion-picture zoos. This was one of the less alarming events. Cecil. B. DeMille directed one day's shooting on *Nan of Music Mountain* (1917) for George Melford, and a blizzard of asbestos snow raged so hard it blew out into the street from the studio, and down on to Hollywood Boulevard and Selma.

CHAPTER ELEVEN
"Our Night to Howl"

Social Life in Hollywood: Scandals

"AFTER nine o'clock at night," said Viola Dana, "you could shoot a cannon off on Hollywood Boulevard and never hit anybody." What little night life there was occurred at the Hollywood Hotel. This handsome building, designed in the Mission style, dominated the little town, and exercised a magnetic influence over the lives of the picture people. Actors would book in until they had located a suitable house for rent; months later, they found themselves still ensconced. The hotel symbolised the impermanence of the new industry. Most people felt they would soon be sent back to New York. No one expected the movies to last.

"The big night," said Viola Dana, "was Thursday night. They used to clear the lobby and we had a dance. Everybody used to look forward to that night. There was an old gal that ran the hotel, a Mrs Hershey, and she was a regular dowager, black ribbon and all that sort of thing. And I want to tell you, there was nothing that went on in that hotel that she didn't know about. She had an eagle eye, and there was no drinking at these dances, or anything like that. It was a case of everybody back to their own room, too!"

The Vernon Country Club was a favourite night spot—well outside Hollywood—but some of the stars looked so young, indeed were so young, that they weren't allowed in. "It was a small community then," said Viola Dana, "and we all knew each other. If we went to a party, it wasn't to be seen or for publicity, it was to have fun. Saturday night we'd go to the Ship Cafe or the Sunset Inn, and that was our night to howl. Because we were a bunch of kids having fun, and we didn't think so much about being elegant."

"Everybody loved everybody," said Adela Rogers St Johns. "There were love affairs going on, and everybody had an excitement about the whole thing that I've never seen since. None of us knew even vaguely what we were doing. None of us knew what this picture business had come to; the greatest form of art and entertainment the world has ever known was put together there for a while. It didn't last long, but it was great, and here we were, right in the middle of this goldfish bowl, with everybody beginning to look at us."

At first, the gaze from the outside world was warm and friendly, even rather shy. The fans found nothing but pleasure in the films, and in this first stage of their love affair with the movies, they wanted to hear no evil about their favourites. Scandal, the staple diet of the yellow press, appeared to be totally absent from the arcadian atmosphere of Hollywood. Beneath the surface, of course, life went on as it did in any other small town. People talked. Telephone operators listened in to calls and spread the gossip. As early as 1912, a group of Keystone actors, about to be arraigned on a charge of contributing to the delinquency of a minor (a sixteen-year-old girl), were hustled over the Mexican border by Mack Sennett. The rest of the Keystone outfit joined them, and films were made 'on location' at Tia Juana as a cover. The year before, a more

serious event had occurred; director Francis Boggs was killed by Frank Minematsu, a Japanese gardener, driven to a breakdown by all the noise at the Selig studio in Edendale.

Scandals were withheld from the public until after the war, and even then it took a series of mysterious deaths to wear down the barrier. 1920 was the year in which a clutch of misadventures occurred. Two young Griffith players died: Clarine Seymour, due to play in *Way Down East,* died during emergency surgery; Robert Harron died of a bullet wound. A story was concocted that a loaded revolver had fallen out of his pocket and the jolt had set it off. Harron had been left out of the cast of *Way Down East,* and the girl he hoped to marry, Dorothy Gish, had chosen another man. Donald Crisp told me that Harron had borrowed a pistol from the property room, and shot himself with 'blank' cartridges made of soap. These disintegrated under normal circumstances, but Harron fired them at point-blank range into his stomach. Jack Pickford's wife, Olive Thomas, died in a Paris hotel this same unhappy year—it looked like suicide but was said to be an accident.

In September 1921, a death occurred in the movie colony which could not be so easily explained away.

"I was making a picture," said Viola Dana, "doing night shots, and using Roscoe Arbuckle's garage and bedroom. At 11 o'clock, Roscoe came in with Sid Grauman (theatre owner) and Joe Schenck (Arbuckle's producer). Roscoe said 'How much longer are you going to be, Vi?' I said, 'Not much longer.' His secretary was there, and he said, 'Vi, can you spend the night here with Katherine?' I said, 'Yes, I don't have to work very early tomorrow.' 'Fine,' he said. 'Now listen, kids. I have to go up to San Francisco. I can't tell you why. But for God's sake don't die on me.'

"We thought that was very strange, but we thought no more about it until the next day, when we saw the papers. Then, of course, we knew exactly what he meant."

Newspapers across the world carried the message: ARBUCKLE HELD FOR MURDER.

Roscoe 'Fatty' Arbuckle was the world's favourite comedian, next to Charlie Chaplin (who was soon due for his own share of scandal). With Chaplin, he shared the affection of children, and the dislike of certain adults; Chaplin's comedy was considered 'vulgar', but Arbuckle's was even earthier. His two-reelers were tremendously successful, and he signed a contract to make features for Adolph Zukor at the salary of three million dollars over three years.

The first feature selected for Arbuckle was, inexplicably, a Western called *The Round Up,* which his namesake, Maclyn Arbuckle, had made famous on the stage. There was very little comedy in *The Round Up.* "It was a disaster," said Joseph Henabery, who directed some of his other features. "Exhibitors rated it 29%—which was nothing. Arbuckle wanted to go back to two-reel pictures. But he had this contract and he had to stay."

The worst fate for a big star lay in those long-term contracts. If he sustained his initial success, he was safe, but as soon as the figures fell, producers searched for ways of dropping him. The standard method was to put him in cheap pictures; the star usually got the message and bought his way out of the contract. Arbuckle rallied with *Brewster's Millions* but he flopped again with *Crazy to Marry*, *Dollar-a-Year Man* and *Travelling Salesman*. For Arbuckle's raunchy style had been toned down; it was closer to light comedy than the knockabout slapstick his audiences loved him for. Paramount forced him to make them so fast—three at once—that the quality suffered.

Arbuckle held a party at the St Francis Hotel, in San Francisco, on Labour Day—September 5, 1921. Among those present was an actress called Virginia Rappe (pronounced Rap-pay). She was taken ill and died four days later. Arbuckle was charged with raping the girl and murdering her.

If other scandals had been successfully suppressed, why was this one so energetically exploited? One reason was that the tragedy had occurred well outside Hollywood—in San Francisco, a city very concerned about its reputation. San Francisco was the headquarters of William Randolph Hearst, the newspaper tycoon, a man who would reveal the private life of his closest friend if it made news. Hearst had been dabbling in the movies (in the East), trying to promote his protégée, Marion Davies, and getting little support from the public and the movie industry.

"Hearst was instrumental in wanting the motion picture industry in Northern California (i.e. San Francisco), and instead it settled in Southern California," said Viola Dana. "I think that was part of his motive in crucifying Arbuckle."

Hearst crucified Arbuckle for another reason—circulation. Newspapers had boosted their circulation by writing about the stars—and most of it had been idolatry. But tabloid newspapers had been introduced in 1919, and they depended on sex and scandal. Hearst was gratified by the Arbuckle scandal; he said later that it had sold more newspapers than any event since the sinking of the *Lusitania*.

But why were the fans now so hungry for blood, having idolised their favourites for so long? In 1921, America was in the grip of the post-war slump. Ordinary people were finding life very hard. The movie publicity machine had once been at pains to show film favourites living comfortably, but not too differently from middle-class people. Mention was seldom made of salaries. Then, during the war, a campaign was conducted against Charlie Chaplin for accepting a million dollar salary instead of enlisting. Mary Pickford and her mother fought constantly for an even higher salary than Chaplin. While the public was attracted to the movies to see what qualities were worth such astronomical sums, the financial revelations inevitably led to a change in their attitude.

Rob Wagner quoted a studio head in his 1918 book *Film Folk*: "When a woman who has been working over a tub of suds all day goes to see Mary play a pathetic little part in rags, she is emotionally touched, but when she learns that this same child is earning twelve thousand dollars a week—two thousand dollars a day!—she is made very resentful. There is a natural indignity in the distribution of the goods in this world; but when a mere slip of a girl draws wages of fifty thousand dollars a month, the underpaid woman will never quite like her the same."

This psychology was not borne out by the events of later years, when the fans expected their favourites to live like royalty, receiving them as such upon their appearances in public. But these were the years of adjustment. While respect for individual initiative survived the revelations of absurdly high salaries, new standards were placed upon behaviour, rather as though the fans were saying, "If you earn that much, you'd better be worth it."

Roscoe Arbuckle's life was paraded before the public by the Hearst press, which dug up every rumour, and trumpeted them as fact: an image of a dissolute roué, bleary eyed from bootleg booze, was thus well established before the unfortunate man's first trial.

The catalyst of the affair was a sinister lady, Mrs Maude Delmont, otherwise known as 'Madam Black', who had brought Virginia Rappe to the party.

"She would provide girls for parties," said Bobby Rose, "and she ran a badger game. She'd get one of these young girls in on a party. and have her claim that a producer or director had tried to rape her. Because in those days, they had open house, almost. Even tourists would come in on the big Saturday night parties. So she'd break in on these parties with these girls and try and frame someone."

Maude Delmont swore out a murder complaint to District Attorney Matthew Brady, who must have been beside himself with excitement. An intensely ambitious man, he planned to run for Governor of California. Here, presented to him in the most sensational terms, was the scandal of the century—an apparently open-and-shut case. Arbuckle, said Delmont, had dragged Virginia Rappe to his bedroom at the height of a drunken party. He had locked the door, and despite her pitiful screams, he had brutally raped her.

Once over his initial excitement, D.A. Brady realised his chief witness had a screw loose. She testified at the inquest, but even the Grand Jury suspected something and reduced the charge of murder to one of manslaughter. Significantly, Brady never allowed his star witness to give evidence again.

Deprived of the whole basis of his case, Brady reverted to threats, suppression of evidence, and outright lies to secure a conviction. For, in his campaign against a Hollywood star, he sought stardom himself.

The public judged the case from the evidence of screaming headlines. Thus began for Roscoe Arbuckle an ordeal which would last for the rest of his life. The long-smouldering resentment against Hollywood exploded. Women's groups across the country rose up in fury. Women stormed the courthouse, demanding the ultimate punishment. His wife rushed to his defence—and was shot at outside the courthouse. Arbuckle's friends were forbidden to give evidence on his behalf, lest their own careers be damaged.

"I tried very hard to be a character witness for Roscoe," said Viola Dana. "I thought a great deal of this man—he was a darling. But Joe Schenck said, 'No, no, no. We don't want your name mentioned in any way that might be injurious.' Because my pictures at that time were making a lot of money."

The defence made a deliberate policy of keeping Hollywood people at arm's length—feeling that the jury was prejudiced enough against such people already. Zukor was obliged to hire top lawyers on Arbuckle's behalf, but otherwise he did little to help. Arbuckle's salary was stopped from the day of his arrest, on the grounds that he was in breach of contract for not appearing for work. Arbuckle's films were withdrawn, and replaced by those of another Zukor star—someone whose innocence could never be brought into doubt, Mary Miles Minter.

During the first trial, several startling facts became known. Virginia Rappe—painted by the Press as Purity herself—proved to have a history of abortions. She suffered from an illness which grew worse when she drank and she drank heavily at the party. David Yallop has written of the trial in *The Day the Laughter Stopped*; his researches reveal a doctor's report that Virginia Rappe had not been attacked in any way. That report was not given at the trial. Yallop is convinced that Rappe died from a mishandled abortion—for she died not in a hospital, but in a maternity home.

The trial was deadlocked. One member of the jury, a woman friend of Brady, insisted that Arbuckle was guilty and she wouldn't change her opinion "till hell freezes over". One man kept her company.

Zukor brought in another lawyer. He tried to secure the services of the great Earl Rogers, but Rogers could not take on the case (and died shortly afterwards).

"Father said, 'They will make it very tough for him, because of his weight,'" said Adela Rogers St Johns. "'The idea of a man of that enormous fatness being charged with the rape of a young girl will prejudice them, even just the thought of it.'"

The scandal caused profound embarrassment to the film colony. The industry was as dependent upon the family audience as television is today. And what disturbed the studio heads was the combined power of the Catholic church, women's clubs and reform groups. These organisations could effect a boycott that would cripple the industry.

The producers felt they had done all they could do for Arbuckle. Now they had to protect their overall investments. They approached a figure from the world of politics to act as an umbrella against the thunderstorm of criticism.

Will H. Hays was the current postmaster-general. Aside from organising newsreels to boost Warren Harding's chances at the polls, Hays had no knowledge of motion pictures. Yet he was to have more influence on their development—or retardation—than any single figure since Thomas Edison.

While Hays went into a metaphorical desert to consult with his conscience, Arbuckle faced his second trial. The defence thought they had it sewn up. Two of the key prosecution witnesses had disappeared, and there was still no sign of Delmont. Arbuckle was not even called upon to give evidence. The jury, however, took this as a sign of weakness. They favoured a verdict of guilty—but once again, they were divided.

The defence was shaken. They had under-estimated the effect of weeks of slander and innuendo. Declaring Arbuckle to be 'the

Dreyfus of America', the defence re-stated the case with clarity and impact at the third trial.

Roscoe Arbuckle was acquitted with an abject apology from the jury—an apology virtually unprecedented in the annals of American law.

"Acquittal is not enough for Roscoe Arbuckle. We feel that a great injustice has been done him . . . There was not the slightest proof adduced to connect him in any way with the commission of a crime. He was manly throughout the case and told a straightforward story which we all believed. We wish him success and hope that the American people will take the judgment of 14 men and women that Roscoe Arbuckle is entirely innocent and free from all blame."

In the face of such a verdict, Adolph Zukor could hardly sustain the embargo on Arbuckle's films. At the same time, he and the other producers wanted to be completely shot of the man whatever the cost. They knew that the public had been convinced of Arbuckle's guilt. So while Zukor announced that the films would return to circulation, the producers all knew what would happen next.

On April 19, 1922, Will Hays made the first major policy decision of his new job. He banned Roscoe Arbuckle from the screen.

*   *   *

If 1920 had been a Year of Misadventure for the film colony, it was a year of mourning for Americans generally. For it was the year in which the Prohibition amendment was ratified, which meant that alcohol was outlawed. Far from benefiting mankind, leading it toward a more sober existence, the law made criminals of the general public. Thanks to Prohibition, an appalling number of people were condemned to death; they had purchased illicit liquor from gangster-owned operations, and some of it was poisonous. Certain kinds of 'whiskey' caused total blindness. Prohibition brought gangsterism to Hollywood.

"I lived next door to the best bootlegger in town," said Karl Brown. "In fact, he was the Al Capone of the Hollywood area and there was very little difficulty about liquor. For one thing, the Los Angeles General Hospital had to have great quantities of absolutely pure grain alcohol for cleaning surgical instruments. It was brought in by the train load. The guardian of the alcohol was not beyond reach, and he was reached.

"Human nature being human nature, arrangements were made whereby all who desired could get five gallon cans of United States Inspected pure grain alcohol, which was the starting point of any liquor you care to make. The favourite was gin, which a nearby druggist manufactured by using the correct amount of alcohol, to which he added distilled water and measured drops of juniper juice, and then, being a very humane man, he added a certain amount of laxative to this mixture so it would not do any permanent harm."

The gangsters established by Prohibition made their mark most distinctly on a later Hollywood; Karl Brown's bootlegger helped to organise strong-arm gangs which the producers employed as strike breakers in the early 1930s.

Gangsterism as a social evil was hard to portray on the screen, because the popular view was so distorted by the Press. The newspapers created folk heroes out of mobsters and lionised them as men of action and of decision, America's equivalent of Mussolini's much-admired blackshirts—men who pitted their lives against the entire force of federal agencies and the bullets of rival gangs. Glittering glamour surrounded them: lavish nightclubs, beautiful and available women, the latest limousines and endless bundles of banknotes. The appurtenances of the upper classes—or film stars—were now adopted by the mobsters, who replaced the languidness of the idle rich with the much more colourful values of the frontier town.

Prohibition was such a vindictive law that reasonable, law-abiding citizens felt obliged to ignore it. The risks attached to drinking added spice to life, and inspired even the most dedicated abstainer. Law-breaking became fashionable. The smartest nightclubs in New York were run by gangsters. Former film star Texas Guinan ran a speakeasy and violence spread through the big cities like a plague, as mobsters fought for supremacy in what became known as the Beer Wars.

The motion picture industry had always been at odds with the liquor corporations, for the nickelodeons wiped out vast numbers of saloons. Early morality films depicted the saloon as a sinful place; an ironic result of all this was the financing of certain censorship lobbies by the breweries.

Prohibition was welcomed by the movies, for it delivered into their hands the hard cases who still haunted saloons. But the industry was under stern orders from Will Hays to exclude wet or dry propaganda, and to handle the matter of drinking on the screen with discretion.

Prohibition was the chief item of discussion in America, but Will Hays knew it would be the storm centre of the next Presidential election. One of the few pictures about prohibition in the early 'twenties was *Those Who Dance*, with Bessie Love and Blanche Sweet, directed by Lambert Hillyer for Thomas Ince (1924). A Federal agent, assigned to combat illicit liquor traffic, joins forces with the gang chief's wife and the sister of the boy who drives the truck, in order to capture the gang. Said *Motion Picture Magazine*: "That great American industry is dealt with here in a story that is decidedly timely. It opens with scenes of the filthy holes where wood alcohol is bottled as imported stuff, and the effects of this poison on a jazz party, which winds up with a realistic auto wreck that kills a girl. The boy driving has been blinded by the hooch."

Drugs as well as alcohol were subject to the law of prohibition; a few years earlier opium was sold openly over the counter of drug stores. In an industry where excess energy was a basic necessity, drugs were valued even more than alcohol. In 1923, one of Hollywood's most popular young stars, Wallace Reid, died of morphine addiction.

"They were making a picture in Oregon called 'Valley of the Giants'," said Karl Brown. "During the production, Wallace managed to hurt a leg in such a way that he was unable to proceed without the greatest possible pain. The picture was nearly finished, but there was no way of shooting round Wally. He just had to be there, in front of the camera. So the company, not wanting to lose the investment entirely, sent the studio doctor, with an ample supply of morphine, to the location, where he injected Wallace to the extent that he could feel no pain whatsoever and he was able to finish the picture. But afterwards, he was thoroughly hooked. Normally he could have been sent to a sanatorium, to a cure, but he was altogether too good box office. There was too much more to be gotten out of Wallace Reid. So in order to keep the services of this most popular of leading men, they kept him supplied with more and more morphine."

Henry Hathaway, then an assistant director, remembered the moment of final breakdown, when Reid was hustled on the set. "He sort of fumbled about, and bumped into a chair, and then just sat down on the floor and started to cry. They put him in a chair, and he just keeled over. They sent for an ambulance and sent him to the hospital." Wallace Reid died, in agony, at the age of thirty, on January 18, 1923. Will Hays said the news "smashed his good works."

Hays had banned all reference to dope on the screen, but in the light of Reid's death and the anxiety of his widow to spread the message, he permitted her to make a propaganda picture about the dangers of narcotics. *Human Wreckage* (1923), directed by John Griffith Wray, and starring Mrs Wallace Reid (Dorothy Davenport) and Bessie Love, opened with this foreword:

'Dope is the gravest menace which today confronts the United States. Immense quantities of morphine, heroine and cocaine are yearly smuggled into America across the Canadian and Mexican borders. The Dope Ring is composed of rings within rings, the inner ring undoubtedly including men powerful in finance, politics and society. But the trail to the "men higher up" is cunningly covered. No investigator has penetrated to the inner circle."

The dope ring was an element in the industry's most distressing catastrophe; the murder of director William Desmond Taylor. One of the leading directors, Taylor had directed both Mary and Jack Pickford, as well as Mary Miles Minter, and it was Miss Minter who seemed mostly closely implicated. Taylor himself was an enigma; at first a theory was put forward that he had been taking on the drug racket single-handed, in the hope of curing his friend, comedienne Mabel Normand, of addiction, but this proved to be desperate publicity in the face of unpalatable evidence.

Taylor was a middle-aged, extremely dignified ex-officer of the British army, who was much in demand as a spokesman for Hollywood organisations, such as the Motion Picture Director's Association, of which he was President at the time of the Arbuckle case. It turned out to everyone's chagrin that Taylor was not his real name, which was William Deane Tanner. He was Anglo-Irish, born in Carlow and educated at Clifton College. He had left his wife and children in New York and started a new life in the West.

The scandal was more damaging even than the Arbuckle trial, for as investigations peeled layer upon layer of corruption and deceit from local society, names of important Hollywood figures were dragged into the papers. The tabloids claimed that Taylor was romantically involved with Miss Minter, with Mabel Normand, *and* with Mary Miles, Minter's mother—an outstanding achievement for a man thought to be a homosexual.

"Everybody knew who shot him," said Adela Rogers St Johns. "There was never any doubt in anybody's mind. We were in the wild and woolly west, and California had some unwritten laws. One was that a man or a woman, a mother or father, had a perfect right to shoot and kill a man who had debauched his or her little girl. It was just accepted, and mostly they didn't even try them." In Miss Minter's contract, a clause stated that no marriage should take place, otherwise the contract was null and void. Miss Minter was contemplating marriage to Taylor. A man was seen leaving Taylor's bungalow, but he walked in a curious way, like a woman.

"I remember Louis B. Mayer saying to me, "said King Vidor. 'If this keeps up there won't be any motion picture industry.' "They were anxious to suppress the whole thing. I think one of Hays' jobs was to keep them from pursuing the case. They'd rather sacrifice Taylor than sacrifice the whole industry."

Paramount was extremely embarrassed, for all the big scandals—Arbuckle, Reid and Taylor—centred around Paramount employees.

"Somebody at the studio had a bright idea," said Karl Brown. "Instead of giving them one or two red herrings, give them a multiplicity of them. Let them leap into the saddle and gallop off in all directions. I don't know of anyone in Hollywood who could have been connected with Bill Taylor who was not implicated in this murder. I honestly believe that the Virgin Mary herself would have been pulled into this thing if she'd been around at the time."

Some of those who dismiss the idea of the mother killing Taylor suggest that Mabel Normand did it. Mary Miles Minter, in this fantasy, comes to visit Taylor, finds the place empty, and sees an open book on his desk. She picks it up and kisses it, leaving the imprint of her lips upon the page. Mabel Normand, calling on Taylor later that evening, spots the incriminating page and shoots Taylor while embracing him. To reverse this theory, the girlfriends can exchange places. But the flaw is that each would have to pack a pistol, anticipating a revelation of infidelity.

While we were in Hollywood, I tried to persuade Mary Miles Minter to give us an interview. She steadfastly refused, but over the telephone, she spoke of the case: "So much hogwash has been written to make money. For instance, in Adela Rogers St Johns' book called 'The Honeycomb' there is a chapter in which she says that she has in her hands the famous pink panties—after that it grew to be a nightgown—embroidered with butterflies and the initials MMM. Well, my mother bought my undergarments and I can imagine her having my initials embroidered anywhere—on an undergarment, or a nightgown. Yes, I can imagine that! It has its comical aspects, but it had occurred to me to demand to see this famous nightgown. It surely must have been kept in the archives, along with whatever was in Mr Taylor's possession in his desk. A few years ago, some police officers came by next door, and I asked them if they would go down and see. Those men did look up the exhibits, and they found Mr Taylor's British officer's jacket—which he was wearing that night—but there wasn't any nightgown. And yet I read of this thing for years—Mary Miles Minter's famous pink nightgown. I marvel to this day where it arose. Whence came the nightgown? What they did find was a handkerchief. It was fashionable in those days for people to give each other handkerchiefs with their whole name embroidered across one corner. Well, one time I had something in my eye, and I was trying to get it out and Mr Taylor said 'Here, take a real handkerchief, not that little dab of lace you have there.' It was a tiny bit of Irish linen surrounded by delicate net—the whole thing was no more than a few inches square. So I said, fair exchange is no robbery, you take this one and I'll take yours. Therefore, it was found at his desk. But that's the only initialled thing I ever had in my life that I left with anybody. As for underwear, it's a joke, laughable and tragic and pathetic."

"Oh, we kept having scandals right along," said Adela Rogers St Johns. "If you throw into one small town and one small industry, the people who can impress the world with their drama, their sex appeal, with their love making, with all of the big emotional, dramatic things that can happen, and you put them all together in one little bowl, you're going to have some explosions. I'm only surprised we had so few."

left] "The grand old Hotel Hollywood," said the original caption in *Photoplay*, "filmland's first and most famous inn, on a busy licentious afternoon. Note the orgy in progress on the lawn."

above] "It is a sad commentary on the cinema centre," wrote a journalist, "that it is impossible for a group of fairly intelligent and decidedly adult people to amuse themselves without resorting to a game."

Viola Dana described the social life of Hollywood at this period as, "a bunch of kids, having fun". William S. Hart could hardly be described as youthful, but the atmosphere of charming lunacy has apparently transformed him; here he provides support for three girls from the Ince studios, Louise Glaum (who usually played vamps), Enid Markey and Margery Wilson, 1917.

"FATTY" ARBUCKLE IN PARAMOUNT-ARBUCKLE COMEDIES

S 271654 R

left] Roscoe Arbuckle was not only a top flight comedian, he was also a skilled comedy director. He trained Buster Keaton in the art of making films—and Keaton became arguably the finest comedy director in the business. Arbuckle's comedies were earthy and vulgar, even more so than Mack Sennett's—therein lay their charm for juvenile audiences all over the world. When he was placed under contract by Paramount, for features, the company smoothed away the vulgarity, and cast him in the kind of straight, light comedy that anyone could have done. Predictably, Arbuckle's popularity at the box-office slackened. Paramount became alarmed. When the news broke about the murder, Paramount might well have harboured thoughts of dumping him. As it was, they did little to help him. When Will Hays raised the ban on Arbuckle in December 1922, Paramount sustained the embargo on his films.

above] Roscoe Arbuckle being arraigned, September 17, 1921, in San Francisco. Had this picture been set up for a movie, had all the participants been carefully cast, it could carry no greater sense of guilt and accusation. Yet Arbuckle was innocent, and the jury at the third trial acquitted him with a fulsome apology.

139-82

left] Bessie Love prepares a dose of morphine—a scene from *Human Wreckage* (1923), a film which reflected the industry's grave anxiety about the drug problem. It was inspired by Wallace Reid's losing battle against drugs. After his death, his wife, Dorothy Davenport, made *Human Wreckage* for the Thomas Ince studios, with the co-operation of the Los Angeles Anti-Narcotic League, and featured police chiefs, narcotic agents and civic leaders. (Regrettably, the film has been lost.)

Wallace Reid is an actor due for rediscovery. He had an endearing sense of fun and enormous charm. He was in the front rank of stardom when he died from drugs in 1923. Drugs were regarded as a grave problem even in the 'twenties, but poor Wallace Reid did not take to them for the fun of it. Like many soldiers, he was given morphine by a doctor to deaden the pain of an injury. The injury was sustained in the service of Famous Players–Lasky (Paramount), a company which had the dubious distinction of employing all the principal personalities involved in the scandals of the early 'twenties. (The scene above is from *The World Champion* (1922).)

CHAPTER TWELVE

The Cleavage Crisis

The March of Censorship

Following the Arbuckle scandal, the industry faced a crisis. Censorship bills were pending all over the country, and organisations of power, such as women's clubs, were up in arms. Will Hays, then the postmaster-general in Harding's cabinet, was approached to become the Czar of the Movies. This is his last cabinet meeting before taking up his post. Hays worried himself into the job. He worried that the reform of the movies might lead to the same result as the reform of alcohol. Perhaps for this reason, he adopted a soft approach, trying to win the industry over to his idea of self-censorship, rather than imposing penalties. It was the alternative of wholesale censorship—differing in every state and city—that brought the industry round to the Hays formula.

right] The kind of film that made censorship inevitable. An Essanay production of 1918, directed by Arthur Berthelet.

George K

I, MARY

Men W
Made

AT ALL FIRST CLASS PICT

VAN NICE

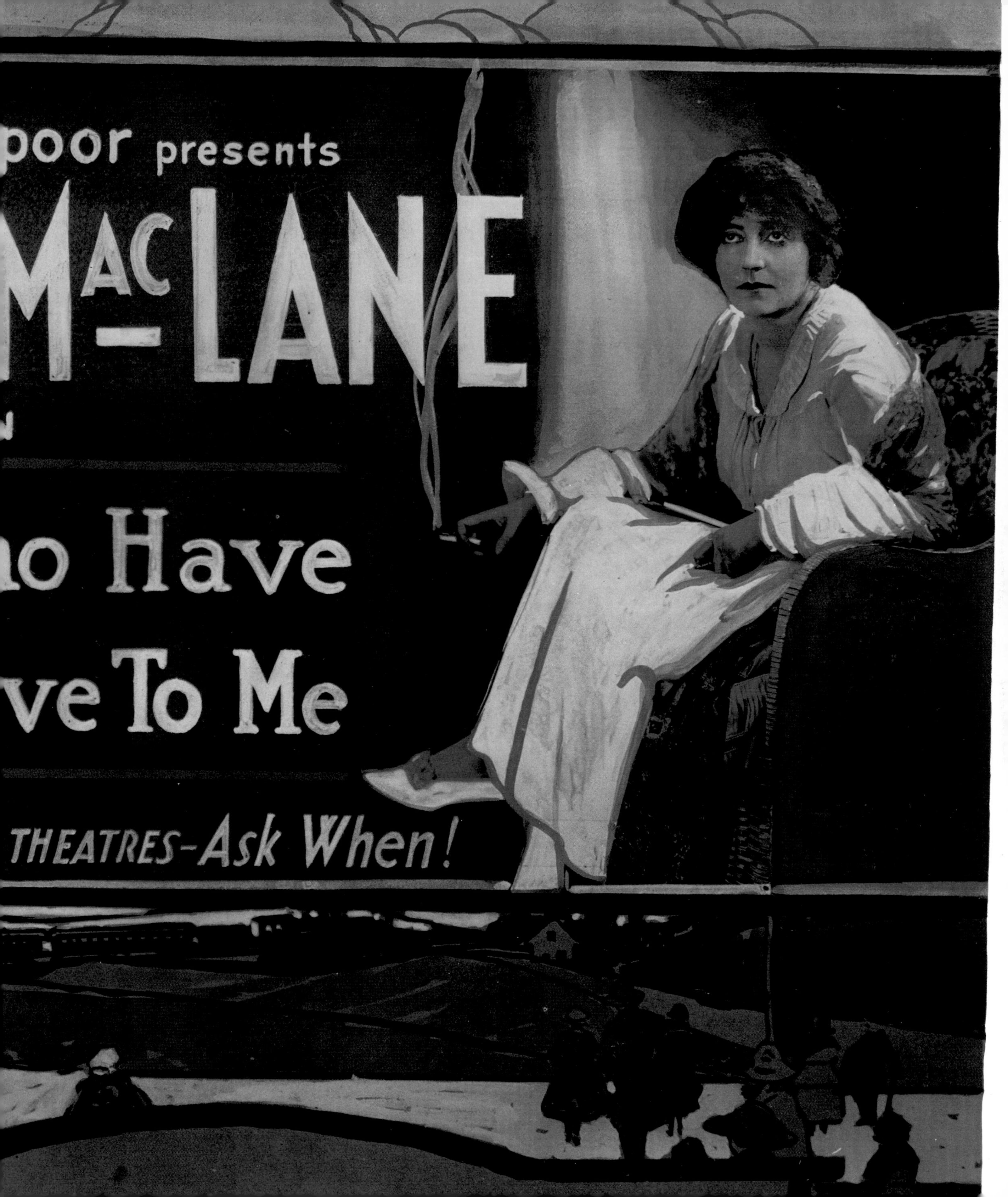
poor presents
MacLANE
no Have
ve To Me
THEATRES–Ask When!

Audrey Munson was chosen to pose for the figure on the memorial coin of the World's Fair at San Francisco in 1915. The newspapers exploited her as the girl with the ideal figure. She was signed by the American Film Company, and Clifford Howard was instructed to write a scenario which would reveal Miss Munson to the public, and at the same time disarm the censors.

"I hit upon the title *Purity*. Whatever may be said of the outcome as a production of art, it fulfilled the company's expectations. It was the most costly film they had turned out, yet by the end of the year they were half a million dollars to the good. Some towns forbade it, and others frankly welcomed it. Critics unmercifully roasted it, and critics enthusiastically praised it. Sermons were preached about it—pro and con. It was the first time I had ever had a hand in the creating of a sensation, and I have never contributed to another."

right] "I wear twenty-eight costumes," said Betty Blythe, of her part as *The Queen of Sheba* (1921), "and if I put them on all at once, I couldn't keep warm." This sort of scene continued to appear in American films after the arrival of Hays—but only in European versions. Cleavage of any sort was forbidden under Hays.

Cecil B. DeMille rode over the Hays formula with cynical ease. He played to the gallery with *Manslaughter* (1922), a film about a crusading District Attorney, which went into production shortly after Hays took over. The D.A. was a Will Hays figure who compared the wild parties of the 'twenties to Roman orgies— providing an ideal opportunity for DeMille to illustrate the comparison as graphically as possible, just to show how shocking they were. The D.A. (Thomas Meighan) also doubled as Attila the Hun, riding down the revellers, in case Mr Hays had any lingering objections.

Scenes like this were extremely rare once the Hays Formula was
established—and they remained extremely rare until the Production
Code lost its power. This brothel appeared in Monta Bell's *Man,
Woman and Sin* (1927); John Gilbert can be seen, with a girl on his
lap, in the background. The black pianist adds an authentic touch.

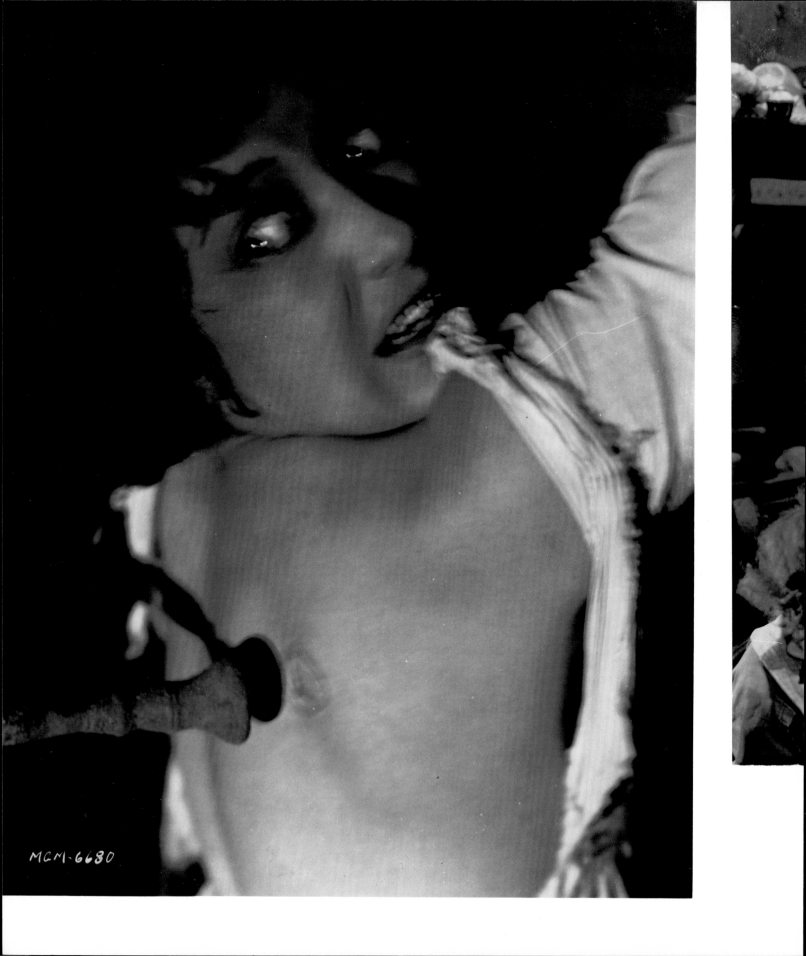

MGM-6680

left] Violence was discouraged by the Hays Office, but this scene had strong precedents. Fannie Ward had been branded in *The Cheat* (1915), Pola Negri in the 1922 remake, Barbara Castleton in *The Branding Iron* (1920) and now Aileen Pringle in the remake of that, *Body and Soul* (1927).

The casual violence of films like *The Penalty* (1920), which remains one of Lon Chaney's best pictures, was discouraged by the Hays Office, and scenes like this largely disappeared from the screen—except in European films.

More often than not, violence became a matter of suggestion
under the Hays Formula. Above, Gloria Swanson in the flashback
scene from *Bluebeard's Eighth Wife* (1923) directed by Sam
Wood, photographed by Al Gilks. On the right, Lon Chaney as
Sergei in *Mockery* (1927), directed by Benjamin Christensen and
photographed by Merritt Gerstad.

impossible for lesser talents to reach the rank of first feature. To attract attention, one athletic young actor called himself William Fairbanks. A stunt man, saddled with the name of Sylvester Metzetti, changed it to Talmadge, thus associating himself with the Talmadge family, Norma and Constance Talmadge being aristocrats of Hollywood. Richard Talmadge was so skilful a stunt man that he should have reached stardom through sheer muscle power, but he was condemned to remain below the surface of success, contributing to the success of others.

"On *The Queen of Sheba*," said Harvey Parry, "a soldier had to swing across from one wall to another. Each time the stunt was tried, the stunt man was hurt, and hurt bad. Carl Harbaugh directed this sequence—a real rough, tough guy. 'Get me Metzetti,' said Harbaugh. Richard Talmadge comes in, takes one look at the thing and says, 'It can't be done.' Harbaugh was furious. 'Give me a toga and a wig and I'll do it myself.' He did—he broke his hip, his collar bone and cut himself up pretty bad. And while he was lying there, Richard Talmadge walked over and said, 'See, you sonofabitch, I told you it couldn't be done.'"

Talmadge's reputation brought him to the attention of Douglas Fairbanks. Fairbanks, regarded as the finest athlete in pictures, was renowned for doing all his own stunts. Yet even he used stunt men. He used them to refine the stunt—so he could watch them, learn from them and then do it himself. But some stunts were filmed in such long shots that it was pointless for Fairbanks to do them— pointless and risky.

As Allan Dwan, director of *Robin Hood* and *The Iron Mask*, said "Of course, when Doug did any of his stunts, he was essentially graceful. That's one thing he struggled for, and I insisted upon. There was never to be any evidence of an effort on his part. Now, when I did them for him—to show him what was expected—I was necessarily awkward. I weighed maybe forty pounds more than he did, although I was his height. I did it by sheer muscular push, while he did it gracefully. If I struggled through the air, he floated through the air. Everything we did was based on a measurement of his reach. Never did he reach with a great effort. Heights of tables, heights of stair risers—we had stairs specially built so he would gracefully go up and down them—no effort. Anybody else would be stretching. What we were after in all the stunts was grace and agility—like a ballet dancer."

Fairbanks had to learn skills far more complex than the basic gymnastics of most stunt men. Apart from fencing and boxing, he had to learn the art of the bullwhip, the bolas—a rope implement used by gauchos—and medieval archery. Some of the incidents that occurred when Fairbanks tried out these stunts off camera were strikingly similar to scenes in his pictures. Allan Dwan recalled: "After the New York opening of *Robin Hood*, the press came to talk to Doug at the Ritz Hotel. They wanted photographs, so we went up on the roof, and Doug brought up a 40 lb bow that he used in the picture, with an arrow. The arrows we had in the show were usually tipped, but this one wasn't. Besides, we wanted it to look good. When he pulled it, we wanted you to see that it had a point. So he posed with this thing, and everyone took pictures of Doug with his bow—and it took muscle to pull it—and then, for some

reason I'll never understand, he let go. On top of the Ritz roof, he pulled this thing back and whang!—he let her go. Of course, I turned chilly when I saw this thing going through the air, but I figured it would hit a roof. But what happened? You have to make a cut.

"Over in the light shaft of a building on the East side, sitting on a window sill, was a little Hungarian Jew, sewing buttonholes. His ass was sticking out of the window and the arrow came down and stuck into it. Now you can imagine the man's fright. He figured he'd been attacked by Indians. He ran out of the building hollering his head off, and was finally stopped by a policeman. The newspaper men came round and the next morning in the paper—here's Fairbanks pulling the bow—and here's a man in Bellevue Hospital with a wound in his fanny! So they tied the things together and it cost Fairbanks $5,000 to square the fellow. But he was very nice. He went right down to see him, and he was so proud at what had happened to him, I guess he wanted Fairbanks to autograph the wound. And of course, he's been sitting on that windowsill ever since, waiting for another arrow."

It was the gasp of the crowd that obsessed publicity-hungry Americans, and it was for this, and the subsequent financial reward, that men went so far as to sit for days atop a flagpole. They were sustained by theatres, hotels and department stores, eager for publicity. The most famous flagpole squatter, star of dozens of newsreels, was Shipwreck Kelly, a boxer who fought under the name of Sailor Kelly, fighting so badly that he won his other sobriquet. Kelly began flagpole squatting in 1924, advertising a theatre. Liquids were hauled up by ropes, and Kelly supported himself against high winds and drowsiness with stirrups. In one year, he spent 145 days sitting on flagpoles.

The human fly was an even more alarming phenomenon, bred by the craze for publicity. The sight of Bill Strothers climbing the Brockman Building so horrified Harold Lloyd that he had to hide his eyes, and this reaction gave him the idea for *Safety Last*.

When Lloyd was first established as a front-rank comedian, he was the victim of an accident which all but ended his career. He posed for some publicity stills, one of which was to show Lloyd, holding a mock bomb, with burning fuse. The bomb had a full charge. The explosion shattered the window, cracked the ceiling and laid him up for nine months. He lost the thumb and forefinger of his right hand, and thereafter, in his pictures, he had to wear a special glove. Yet he could not continue as a top comedian unless he went on with the dangerous stunt work he was famous for. Lloyd forced himself back to the peak of condition, rose to even greater popularity, and employed stunt men only for the hardest work.

"We'd build a set," said Harvey Parry, "on top of a fourteen storey building that was maybe two and a half storeys in height right on the edge, facing in towards the roof of the building. When they photographed it, they photographed it in such a way that it looked like it was on the opposite side of the street, and you could see all that traffic underneath.

"If Harold did fall—or if I fell—we'd only fall fifteen feet, and we'd have pads down there. He did most of the work himself, for he was a good athlete, but he only had one hand, and there were some things he couldn't do.

"When they opened *Safety Last* in New York, they had a young kid who was going to climb a building. He was a human fly, and he'd just been married. The dangerous thing about climbing is the dust you find on the ledges. This kid went up and successfully reached the 32nd floor. Nobody knew what happened—he slipped and fell . . . almost at his wife's feet."

The cult of speed which gripped the nation was expressed most eloquently in the growth of aviation. Civil flying had been banned during the war, but with restrictions lifted, ex-government planes were sold for a few hundred dollars, ready crated. The barnstorming boom burst into the headlines. Lt Ormer Locklear was the most charismatic of the show fliers. He won his reputation in the Air Corps, climbing out on the wings of an aircraft to prove they were strong enough to carry extra guns. In 1919, he repeated the stunt for the public and the newsreel cameras, capping it by transferring from one plane to another without a parachute. Locklear was hired for pictures.

Viola Dana was engaged to Locklear, and she experienced virtually every stunt Locklear could perform. "We'd go between telegraph poles and chase our friends down Hollywood Boulevard, and I'd carry a bunch of old lipsticks and I'd throw them—that's how close we'd fly. I think they got after him. He had to leave town on one occasion—he hid out for about a week."

"This Ormer Locklear was a very popular man, a very daring man, and he took all the stars up," said Leatrice Joy. "Every time he came to the studio, I succeeded very tactfully in avoiding him, not because I was scared, but because I wasn't particularly interested. I was having too much fun on earth. He stopped me in the hallway and he said 'I know, you're Leatrice Joy.' I made out I was very weak and about to die, so he would think I wasn't too robust. 'You know,' he said, 'you're the only star who hasn't gone up. Come on

now, let's make a day of it.' So I said, 'All right.' We went up in this little crackerbox, so help me heaven, and we started zooming up. He made an Immelmann curve, then the reverse of it and all those kind of things, and I thought 'I've had enough.' I made some kind of gesture to him—meaning take me down, and he gave me an enthusiastic okay sign. I wondered why he was so happy about taking me down, and all of a sudden, he zoomed up again, and went into the most daring of any of those stunts—the Falling Leaf. You spin down, down, you practically pick buttercups. Then he landed and stopped and picked me up and said, 'Congratulations. You're the only star with guts, Miss Joy. You're the only one who asked for the Falling Leaf.' And I didn't have the courage to say, 'That was my sponge I was throwing in.' "

While making *The Skywayman*, Locklear and co-pilot Milton Elliott were making night scenes over the oilfields of the Wilshire District. Flares had been attached to the plane, which had been painted white, so that the sunlight arcs on the ground would pick it out against the night sky.

"He was supposed to go into a tailspin," said Viola Dana. "He had said to the director, 'Now, when I get down to the level of the oilwells, take the lights off me, and I'll know where I am. I can come out of it.' He went into the tailspin and they never took the lights off, and he crashed into an oil sump. I guess there was practically nothing left of him, because those Jennies were very fragile. I started to run for the plane, and somebody said 'Grab her and take her home.' Whoever took me home, I don't know. All this is very vague to me now, because it was such a shock. But I do remember that my hair started to fall out—I could pull it out in clumps, the shock was so great. I guess I was just kind of crazy. I couldn't believe what had happened. When you're young, those things are very shocking. I don't even like to talk about it."

It is hard to believe anyone could survive this mishap. The unfortunate stunt man is Harvey Parry. The scene was shot on the roof of a hotel in Hollywood. Comedian Earle Foxe was supposed to jump off the roof on to a bathhouse tent, and bounce into the swimming pool. In reality, Harvey Parry jumped off the roof on to a trampoline hidden in the bathhouse tent—and bounced into a fire net. The men holding the fire net were so busy watching Harvey bounce off the trampoline, they did not guess where he would fall. He landed on his back—but was uninjured. The director wanted

another take—and precisely the same thing happened. Harvey landed on his back and had the wind knocked out of him.

"I wouldn't have minded," said Harvey Parry, "but I was standing in for another stunt man—trying to save his job—and they never paid me."

right] This daring plane-to-plane transfer by Ormer Locklear has been photographed from the same spot as *The Terror Trail* (*overleaf*), the top of the Hill Street tunnel.

Studios tried hard to prevent leaks of their trade secrets. They
knew that once a photograph was taken, the chances were it would
appear in some publication. For this reason, photographs revealing
tricks of the trade were discouraged. Which makes these two
pictures all the more remarkable. They show clearly how the
topography of Los Angeles aided the thrill pictures. These sets have
been erected above the Hill Street tunnel. (The Hotel La Crosse in
the background was at 122, South Hill St.) When sound arrived,
such scenes were shot in the studio, against back projection, a
method which effectively muted the realism. The girl on the fire
escape left (it's a dummy in the picture above) is Eileen
Sedgwick, in a Universal serial of 1921, *The Terror Trail*,
directed by Edward Kull.

Harold Lloyd's superlative comedies included only a handful in which he clung from tall buildings, yet he is remembered today mainly as a stunt comedian. He hated heights himself, which was why he set about making these pictures, reasoning that audiences would find them as frightening as he did. He was right—and many people kept their eyes tightly shut during the worst moments. Lloyd did a lot of his own stunts, for he was a good athlete, but there was a limit to the risks he could take. For one thing, he was an expensive star, and an accident to him would cripple the whole

company. For another, he only had one good hand. He lost several fingers of the other when a property bomb exploded during a still photograph session. He wore gloves whenever he could, and the scene above—from *Never Weaken* (1921)—shows him wearing bandages as well as a glove on his right arm. For ordinary scenes, he wore a glove shaped like a hand that concealed the disability from his audience.

The tricky scenes—like the one from *Safety Last* (1923) on the left—were undertaken by stunt men like Harvey Parry.

CHAPTER FOURTEEN

Leave 'em Laughing

Comedy

THE fact that the silent era was one of unparalleled richness in visual comedy has now been generally accepted. The comedies are even used occasionally as a weapon to lambast the dramas (by those who have seen very few silent dramas).

In the same way, the films of Buster Keaton, which are shown quite often, are used to decry the films of Charlie Chaplin, whose best films are less frequently seen (and when they are, the prints are usually invisible).

Chaplin is temporarily out of favour. It has become fashionable to say "I love Keaton, but I don't like Chaplin." Chaplin was very much a man of his time. Keaton, unsentimental and cynical, is more a man of ours. During his career, Chaplin received an extraordinary degree of praise, and audiences therefore expect more from his films than anyone else's. Having been delighted by a Keaton of 1925, they are disappointed that a Chaplin of 1916 is not equally inventive.

It is therefore necessary to explain that without Chaplin there would have been no Keaton—and no Harold Lloyd either.

Chaplin arrived when American comedy films were knockabout farces. Comedies with characterisation had been made—with John Bunny, and Mr and Mrs Sidney Drew—but slapstick was easier to produce, and it guaranteed the laughs. Chaplin's stage work proved he was highly skilled in slapstick—and that was the only reason he was hired. But as he worked before a camera, and began to appreciate its power, he felt compelled to expand the boundaries of film comedy to include all the elements he had learned in his theatrical career—light comedy, mime, pathos . . . As a result, his comedies stood out above all others. His characterisation was so strong that audiences across the world fell in love with him. Nothing he did could displease them, although his vulgarity caused a lot of comment in the Press, and Chaplin was obliged to tone his films down somewhat. But while such vulgarity may have captured the audiences, it was his subtlety that enchanted them. His most prolific period was 1916–17; almost every month, he produced a little masterpiece. These two-reelers—*The Rink*, *The Cure*, *The Immigrant*—changed the face of film comedy. They were so successful that other comedians—and other producers—were forced to take notice of them.

It is taking nothing from Keaton or Lloyd to say that Chaplin built the road along which they swept to success. And Chaplin has paid the price for being a pioneer. His films look old-fashioned beside those of the later comedians, yet the very plainness of his style was effective; he produced exactly the results he wanted.

During the making of this series, David Gill and I had the privilege of seeing some of the films he made for fun at his studio; they were all directed with the same painstaking care he lavished on his regular comedies. When one realises how much he put into his work, it's not surprising he had problems in his private life!

Fashion will change again, and so long as Chaplin's films survive, so will his genius. He was, and he will always remain, the greatest comedian in the history of the motion picture.

*　　*　　*

The cinema quickly learned the attraction of making people laugh. Commercially, comedy could be more profitable than drama, for it cut across the class barrier. People who normally looked down upon the cinema were beguiled by the early trick films, and convulsed by the comedians.

Mack Sennett, the great comedy producer, was embarrassed by the overwhelming praise that greeted him in later life, for, as he freely admitted, "I stole my first ideas from the Pathés". The French company, Pathé Frères, turned out inventive comedies very early in the century which he reproduced and elaborated upon. Sennett had a raucous sense of humour, and a blind spot for subtlety. His comedies were chaotic and ridiculous—which was why, in a tightly disciplined society, so many people loved them.

Sennett had worked with Griffith at the Biograph Company, and he was given the task of directing some of the Biograph comedies. *The Curtain Pole* (1909) was nominally directed by Griffith, but Sennett took the leading role and probably the initiative, for Griffith had little flair for slapstick. The result was a crazy but brilliant little film, inspired by the English, French and the earlier Biograph chase films: it has a freshness about it shared by few other comedies of the period, and it set the pattern for Sennett's future techniques.

"Sennett worshipped Griffith," said Frank Capra. "He'd walk with Griffith from Griffith's home to the Biograph studio every morning, and walk with him back again. He wanted to hear the Master talk, he wanted to listen to every word. He absolutely worshipped him." Sennett must have been greatly pleased, towards the end of the silent era, by a review for *The Goodbye Kiss*, a feature which he personally directed: "It has moments worthy of D. W. Griffith," said *Photoplay*.

"Sennett was a simple yet complex man," said Capra. "He needed butlers in full dress suits around him, and he needed to eat with a black tie. He looked ridiculous with a black tie and his butlers looked ridiculous in their livery. He had a tremendous library of books. When I finally looked at one, the leaves had never been cut. He just bought them by the yard. He had this strange quality of being simple; yet he tried to be sophisticated and as he himself said, he never made it."

If the French comedies were his inspiration, he was sustained by the English music hall. Hal Roach, Sennett's rival as comedy producer, said that a great many of the comedians working for Sennett were English. "The music hall in England produced a great many fine comedians. As far as visual humour is concerned, more of it was produced in England than any place else—particularly in the Karno group."

Sennett made up his mind that the important man at the studio was Mack Sennett and with the imperious air of Griffith, refused to demean himself by securing proper contracts with his employees. As Roach pointed out, he could have had some of the most famous stars in history under his exclusive control—Roscoe Arbuckle, Gloria Swanson, Mabel Normand . . . not to mention that young Englishman from the Karno troupe, Charlie Chaplin. They all worked for him, but they all left him.

At Sennett's company, Keystone, Chaplin was first placed under the direction of Henry 'Pathé' Lehrman, whom he loathed. He was next assigned to Mabel Normand's unit. Mabel was a very beautiful girl, around twenty, who expected to marry Sennett and who was deeply in love with him. She was very loyal, and regarded the opinionated Chaplin, who decried Sennett's methods, as an intruder. Chaplin was also young, and very attracted to Mabel, and he felt hurt by her. He refused to acknowledge her competence, and behaved like the lemon Sennett thought he was. For one scene, Mabel asked him to stand with a hose and to spray the street so that the villain's car would skid. Chaplin remembered the old Lumière film in which a boy steps on a gardener's hose, and when the gardener peers down the nozzle to see what's wrong, he gets a jet of water in his face; he suggested this gag to Mabel, who knew how fast the Sennett comedies had to be ground out. "We have no time," she said. Chaplin refused to play the scene, and sat on the kerb in a sulk. Mabel was taken aback by such behaviour; this was not the spirit she was used to. Eventually, the company returned to the studio, and Chaplin was given a stern dressing down by Sennett, who threatened to fire him. Chaplin considered going back to England. But Sennett received word from the New York office that the Chaplin films were popular; he was obliged to give the new comedian greater creative control. First, he brought about a reconciliation with Mabel Normand, and the three became firm friends.

Chaplin owed as much to the French and British traditions of comedy as Sennett; his characterisation of the impeccably-mannered tramp absorbed elements of the French comedian Max Linder, the first great comic the movies produced. Chaplin grew surprisingly touchy about the supposed influence of other comedians, and none of them appear in his autobiography. But he acknowledged his debt to Linder at the time; one of his little home movies shows Linder's visit to the studio in World War One; they embrace warmly, and each tries the other's routines.

Chaplin's success was an indication of the public's hunger for film comedy—a hunger which increased as the war in Europe grew worse. Chaplin became a true hero of that war, for his work did nothing but good.

If Griffith's *The Birth of a Nation* brought in a new audience, Chaplin was the first to exploit that audience. Which makes it all the more curious why, having played in a highly successful Sennett feature of 1914, *Tillie's Punctured Romance*, he failed to produce a feature of his own until 1921.

When that feature was made, however, Chaplin once again changed the face of film comedy.

The Kid starred Jackie Coogan, who was four years old when he appeared with his father—Jack Sr—in a vaudeville act. Chaplin saw the act, and was so impressed he determined to have Jackie in a picture. But Arbuckle signed him first. Chaplin was dismayed; he knew just how effective the little boy would be opposite the fat man. When it turned out to be a false alarm—Arbuckle was negotiating for the father—Chaplin gratefully brought the boy to the studio and slowly and painfully put the film together. For Jackie Coogan, the film was the experience of his life. He still talks about it with delight. Chaplin was immensely kind and considerate, and his direction of the boy was one of the miracles of the movies.

"The Chaplin studio was unique," said Coogan. "And as he was the only producer on the lot, we had the whole place to ourselves. Sometimes we wouldn't turn a camera for ten days while he got an idea. And when he got an idea, he brought it all together in his mind. He was a brilliant man. Everybody in the motion picture business or any of the arts should be terribly envious of this man because he had it all. He could originate it, he could facilitate it and he was a director; he later scored all his own pictures, and he had the ability to get the most out of people.

"Here you've got a little boy, a waif, he's adopted without the benefit of the law, and he gets sick and the County Orphanage man comes and says, 'He has to go into the hospital. Are you the father?' And he says, 'No . . .' And they try to take me by force to the workhouse, which was practically condemning a child to death in those days.

"I can remember him explaining what he wanted me to do. He started to dramatise it—I saw it in my mind's eye. He was a marvellous story-teller, and he put it on an intensely personal basis, so that when he said 'Camera' and then 'Action!' and the Welfare Worker threw me into this truck, that's when the dam broke. I was really gone. I was torn up. 'I want my daddy.' I was hysterical. If you are going to portray someone being hysterical, you'd better get yourself hysterical, or it's as phoney as a three-dollar bill. You've just got to let everything go. It's just like vacuumising yourself, just letting everything out. In a grown person, I would say frustrations; in a child, I don't know what was let out. But I know I just felt hollow. My head was like a bell that was ringing."

Chaplin's success triggered off a series of imitators. Some were outright mimics, like Billy West, who dressed himself to look exactly like Chaplin and made every effort to duplicate the look of the Chaplin films. Others simply followed in Chaplin's footsteps.

One of these was Harold Lloyd. Beginning in pictures as an extra, with Hal Roach, Lloyd developed into a comedian of the first rank, who seriously rivaled Chaplin at the box-office during the 'twenties. Whereas Chaplin made only three full-length features in that golden decade of comedy, Lloyd made eleven. Chaplin got his start with Sennett; Lloyd was brought to fame by Hal Roach. His characterisation resembled Chaplin's.

"Lloyd was unhappy at being just another Chaplin imitator," said Roach. "We had a guy that did a great drunk, and he came on the set with a pair of glasses without any lenses in them. He looked very funny with these things on, and that's where I got the idea of the glasses for Lloyd. The character was an almost immediate success." Lloyd liked the glasses because he had just seen a film about a deceptively meek, bespectacled parson, who turned into a raging pugilist when the occasion demanded. The simple addition of a pair of glasses enabled Lloyd to break cleanly from the Chaplin influence, and establish himself as an original.

The most precious advantage of the full-length feature, lay in the extra time the comedian had to develop character. Lloyd was obsessed with what he called 'character comedy'. His first full-length production was *Grandma's Boy* (1923).

"Lloyd felt that two sequences in the picture should be done dramatically, without comedy," said Roach. "And so the sequence in which he played his grandfather (in the Civil War) was done straight. The sequence in which he caught the bad man was also done straight. We previewed that in Pasadena, and when we came to the grandfather's sequence, we dropped the audience. It took us another half hour to pick them up. By that time, we'd come to the sequence where he was supposed to catch the bandit—that was done dramatically, and we dropped them again. So we got to the end of the picture and we couldn't pick them up and the preview absolutely died.

"At two o'clock in the morning, I was still arguing with Lloyd. I told him, 'those two sequences must be made funny. To hell with the dramatic idea'. And he lost the argument. I called the writers in the following morning and I said, 'I want every writer to come up with a gag for the grandfather sequence; I want every writer to come up with a gag for the end sequence where they catch the bandit. If you don't come up with a gag, you're fired. And,' I said, 'I will give you the first gag.' I remember it well. That was when Lloyd was trying to catch the bandit. He had a lasso, and he was driving the Ford, and as he went by he threw the lasso at the bandit, missed the bandit and caught a post which pulled him out of the car—so he was alone with the bandit out there."

To his chagrin, Harold Lloyd was labelled as a stunt comedian; the picture of him hanging from a clock seems to be all that people remember. Lloyd has only himself to blame, for he refused to reissue his films, and only towards the end of his life did he release a couple of compilations. How could modern audiences know of his full, amazing range?

Lloyd's features shared many of the same gag-men with the Keaton films, and they had something of the same surface polish. Lloyd was never credited with the direction, but nothing escaped his notice. He had to approve every gag, ever set, every camera angle. He supervised the films as closely as David Selznick supervised *Gone with the Wind*, which is why a director like Teddy Wilde could make two masterpieces for Lloyd—*Kid Brother* and *Speedy*—but nothing much for anyone else.

Lloyd's character altered from film to film. He was an outstanding actor—his facial expressions were so subtle that you sometimes thought that, like Keaton, they never changed. And yet they could convulse you all by themselves—as when he accidentally consumed a perfume-soaked powder puff in mistake for a bun in *For Heaven's Sake* (1926).

Interest in Lloyd is now gaining momentum; his films are in circulation, at least in America, and two fascinating books have been published about him: *Harold Lloyd, the shape of laughter* by Richard Schickel, and *Harold Lloyd, the king of daredevil comedy* edited by Adam Reilly.

Buster Keaton, on the other hand, is well established, and well loved. Fortunately, he was able to live just long enough (he died in 1966) to see the start of his revival. There is such a dearth of visual comedy today that the Keaton films, seen in isolation, seem astonishing. In the silent era, there were so many outstanding comedies competing for attention that the Keatons were not regarded as exceptional. I think audiences then were blind to qualities which have become apparent since. Nevertheless, Keaton as a comedian was rated highly—one just wishes his skills as a film maker had been encouraged for a little longer. But he was essentially a silent comedian, and by the time the silent era was over, he began to lose ground.

"Buster was the original man who came to dinner," said Viola Dana. "He came home one night with my sister and brother-in-law, and he stayed for three years. He became one of the family. My mother was crazy about him—he was like a son to her—and whenever we moved, we figured on Buster.

"Buster came from the stage. He dressed like his father—that funny little pork-pie hat—and when he was a little kid, his father used to pick him up by the scruff of the neck and throw him into the backdrop."

A graduate of this tough school of vaudeville, Keaton came to films as a stunt man of twenty years' experience when he was twenty-three. He was fascinated by the mechanics of film making, by the careful and intricate preparations that went into the ultimate goal of the comedian—a laugh from an audience. He took immense care over such details. His gags were never hit-and-miss. They were calculated with the precision of an engineer's blueprint.

For all his resourcefulness, Keaton was defeated by one sequence from *Seven Chances*. The chase, he felt, was just a chase. There were no outstanding gags. Worse still, there was no climax. Keaton miserably decided he had done all he could do—it was still a dud. He previewed it before an audience, and a few giggles accompanied the chase. Just before the fade-out, the audience erupted in a roar of laughter. "What the hell caused that?" Keaton asked. None of his crew could tell him. They took the picture back to the studio and ran the scene . . . slowly. They discovered their unnoticed gag. A rock had pursued Keaton as he ran down a hill. It had dislodged a couple more rocks, and the three little rocks joined the chase. So the Keaton company shot a totally new sequence—in which Keaton triggers an avalanche of progressively larger stones. For its split-second timing and for its sheer resourcefulness, the sequence deserves the description of masterpiece. He made several more brilliant comedies until his producer, Joseph Schenck, sold him to MGM and his free-wheeling style of comedy was gradually brought to a standstill.

The briefest, and certainly the saddest, career was that of Harry Langdon. Langdon was more of a manufactured comedian than the others. Brought into pictures by Sennett, he was handed over to

144

gagmen Frank Capra and Arthur Ripley.

"Mr Sennett had seen his act with his wife on vaudeville," said Frank Capra, "he had had it photographed, and he brought him to the studio, and turned him loose with all the comics. The Mack Sennett comics just ran faster than anybody—did bigger pratfalls than anybody—and here was this child-like character who took five minutes to wink. Nobody wanted him. But Sennett kept saying, 'You guys all know what he's got. He's got something.' So it came to our turn. Ripley and I looked at the film, and just agreed with everyone else. Ripley said, 'Only God could help that twerp.'

"I had just read *The Good Soldier Schweik*, and the connection between the two was immediate. We asked permission to work on it for a while. We made the picture, and it was a tremendous hit as a two-reeler. A new star was born. A new kind of personality. Innocence was his forte.

"Then he was hired by another studio to make features and I went with him as gag man and finally became his director. The first picture I directed for him was *The Strong Man*, which I thought was very good—and had everything that Langdon could do, and do right.

"He went Hollywood all of a sudden—he suddenly started to wear scarves and bright clothes. He bought a big house, and discovered girls, because he read the wonderful reviews from New York—people went crazy about this man, and he just couldn't handle it. He couldn't handle the renown he was getting. So when we made *Long Pants*, he said, 'I want to do more pathos.' I said, 'No, no—the pathos is in your comedy.' 'How the hell do you know?', he said. 'Do you know more than those critics in New York?' So it ended up—they fired me at the end of *Long Pants* and he edited the picture himself. I don't think it was edited very well, although it had many funny things in it.

"But then he directed himself. Now, his one idea was to equal or supersede Chaplin—in Chaplin's own material. And of course, the minute he got away from his character, he was not Langdon any more. He went downhill very fast, and I didn't see him for years after that. The next time I saw him, I peeped in on a sound stage, and there he was, re-doing a famous gag that we had in *The Strong Man*, in which he carried a woman on his lap, up the stairs, one at a time, backwards. And the director was yelling to him, 'Faster, faster, Harry, for God's sake—faster!' 'Faster' was not the thing to say to Langdon. 'Slower', yes, but not 'faster'.

"Then he went way down to where he couldn't get a job. He worked as an extra* and finally died. I think he died of a broken heart. But he never knew the difference between his own character and Chaplin's. He never knew that Chaplin invented his own character, and could direct himself, because he knew his own character better than anybody else. But Langdon did not invent his own character. It was invented for him. And that he never understood. It was a tragedy."

* He worked on, admittedly in obscurity, as a comedian and gag man, standing in at one point for Stan Laurel when the Laurel and Hardy partnership broke up. He died in 1944.

The talking picture stifled the style of the silent comedians, and only Laurel and Hardy carried it through the next decade. Both were veterans of the picture business—Laurel had been a member of the Karno troupe with Chaplin. "I don't think any two men have worked better than they did," said Hal Roach, their producer. One of their last silents, *Big Business* (1929) had them selling Christmas trees in California. "They needed a bungalow they could wreck," said Hal Roach, "so the location manager made three or four photographs of different bungalows and showed them to the director. The director picked one that happened to belong to someone working at the studio. We made a deal with this man and his wife to go on vacation for a month. While they were gone, we would make the picture, wreck their house, pay him for the use of it and guarantee to put it back in the same condition as it was before.

"On his way to the location, the director had this picture in his hand. There was a house a block away from the house we had, that looked exactly the same. The director said, 'This is the house,' and pulled in. The crew got off, unloaded their things and finally the assistant director said, 'The key doesn't open the door.' He said, 'It makes no difference. We're going to break the lock anyway.' And they went to work. They cut all the trees, they broke all the windows, they broke the front door, they broke everything to do with the house. They had about two more days to go and a car pulled up in front of this house with a man, his wife and two children. The wife practically fainted, the man the same. And that was the first time we found out we were doing this at the wrong house."

In this scene, James Finlayson (right) has just smashed Laurel and Hardy's windscreen, and Laurel is trying to bite his ear, by way of retaliation. The house, soon to be wrecked, stands behind them.

146

CHAPTER FIFTEEN

Cult of the Personality

Stardom

THE age of ballyhoo—the roaring twenties—when fan worship, whipped into searing passion by a gigantic publicity machine, reached epidemic proportions. Personal appearances caused riots. And when a great star died, some of his fans followed him into the next world.

It is hard to believe that only a few years earlier, actors were anonymous. The first decade of the century was the only time in the industry's history that it operated successfully without stars. A few names were known—the Trust had players like John Bunny and Maurice Costello—but film manufacturers were agreed on the folly of duplicating theatrical stardom, with salaries cresting waves of imbecility.

The independents, however much they agreed with that principle, needed every weapon they could lay their hands on to break the power of the Trust. When the newspapers ran a report of the death of the 'Biograph Girl', in 1910, the anonymity of players was breached. For the Biograph Girl was at last identified as Florence Lawrence. "Deep regret" was premature, for Miss Lawrence was very much alive, having been lured from the Trust by the shrewd, publicity-conscious Carl Laemmle, who had named her the IMP Girl and had almost certainly leaked the fiction himself. Now he could splash advertisements denying what he called, "the blackest and silliest lie circulated by the enemies of the IMP"—and make the star's name even more widely known. He staged a personal appearance for Miss Lawrence in St Louis, and IMP publicity insisted that the crowds went berserk and tore strips off her clothes for souvenirs. The press reports of the time indicated a somewhat more sedate reception, but as publicity men had long been aware, the wilder the story, the greater its circulation. The star system was based on myth and imagination, and through ingenious fabrication it would flourish.

The Biograph held out against the idea of revealing their players until 1913. The Griffith players, anonymous though they were, became the best loved actors on the American screen. Mary Pickford inherited the title of Biograph Girl after Florence Lawrence's departure, and her intimate, naturalistic and humorous style captivated the public. They were convinced that her screen personality was her own.

"When Mary Pickford was with the Griffith company," said Blanche Sweet, "they used to call her, in the titles, Little Mary. It was the first time anybody's name had been personally used at Biograph. The answer to that was that she got an offer from an independent company for more money, and she accepted it, and the Biograph Company said, 'Ah, you see what happens if you use a real name. Nobody's name must be known in the company—no names used at all.' But Britain demanded to know who the Biograph people were. Biograph's answer went only half way. They put our photographs on a poster, and called us all by British names. My name was Daphne Wayne."

Some of the other companies were reluctantly obliged to follow Laemmle's example, or risk losing players anxious for recognition and more money. The first stars were introduced in a diffident manner: a 1911 preview, *Ruth Roland, Kalem Girl*, implied that the actress was a refined young lady of charm and breeding. Such an approach appealed to the latent snobbery of the Nickelodeon audiences. The later technique of establishing the star as a goddess would simply have alienated them.

The impatient men who ran the business could not wait for new stars to develop. They set out to attract established stars from the theatre. Zukor had already introduced Bernhardt and set the style for other companies. In 1915 the Lasky Feature Play Company brought opera star Geraldine Farrar to Hollywood.

"When Geraldine Farrar came out," said Agnes de Mille, "there was a great to do about her in Hollywood. It was the first time an opera singer of her stature had come out. She had her whole entourage, her own maid and her own hairdresser, her own manager and she had her own private dressing room. Everybody adored her, particularly the cowboys; 'Our Gerry' they called her, and they gave her a beautiful mirror at the end of *Joan the Woman*, with the fleur-de-lis on it, and all their names—every grip, every cameramen, everyone. They worshipped her. I don't think I've met a star in my life who had that effect on people."

The theatrical era of American films was over by 1916. The general consensus of historians is that the theatrical experiment was a complete flop. But that can hardly have been the case. The moving picture by 1916 had overtaken the theatre and vaudeville as the staple public entertainment. It had forced the closure of theatres across the country. It had ravaged theatrical receipts, caused the breakdown of the roadshow system, and it had led to the legitimate stage erecting its last bastion, like a circle of covered wagons, on Broadway.

The theatrical stars were merely a means to that end, helping in the destruction of their own business. The movies consumed them as they consumed every kind of public figure, from impeached politicians to rodeo heroes. If they brought in the paying public, that's all that mattered. The moment the box-office faltered, they were dropped. In any case, most had accepted film work on a short-term basis.

Film players had not been blind to the vast salaries paid to the stage stars, and in this respect, producers had been inordinately shortsighted. Sir Herbert Beerbohm Tree was paid $100,000 for six weeks work. Conscious of their own power, the film stars demanded similar salaries, Mary Pickford displaying an unnerving knowledge of her own value as a star. Adolph Zukor excited her with his plans for Famous Players, and with her mother, Charlotte Pickford, acting as agent, Mary Pickford squeezed from him a salary of $500 a week. For 1914, that was astonishing enough, but she quickly forced the figure up, and up—way beyond what anyone was earning in the theatre.

"Mary Pickford was the best known woman that has ever lived," said Adela Rogers St Johns, "and the picture business, when it made great money, really came in first with Mary Pickford. Her pictures were the first ones that made these vast fortunes."

Zukor knew that to control the stars meant controlling the industry, and he fought hard to keep Pickford, offering her a vast sum to stop work—anything to prevent her falling into the hands of his competitors. As historian Benjamin Hampton said, "She was the only member of her sex to become the focal point for an entire industry." Pickford left Zukor because she was not granted the right to approve the script. She signed with First National in 1919 for $675,000 a year, plus fifty per cent of the gross. The only male stars offering a similar drawing power were Chaplin and Douglas Fairbanks.

Fairbanks had come from the Broadway stage—one of the few stage actors to become a success in pictures. "He fell in love with the film medium," said Douglas Fairbanks Jr, "because he was able to tell his story in mime. He and Chaplin had a lot in common. Behind the improbable, little-boy adventures made almost believable, with the optimism and good cheer which were part of his philosophy, was the thought that if you had enough confidence in yourself, and were quick-witted enough, everything would come out all right."

Fairbanks and Pickford were united artistically with Charlie Chaplin and D. W. Griffith in an organisation appropriately named United Artists, which gave them independence from the control of producers and the demands of exhibitors. They set out to make pictures to the best of their ability, and they would let the public judge them on their merits. They would not bolster them with the block booking system employed elsewhere—in which exhibitors were forced to take ten unimportant pictures in order to secure one super-production. A series of beautifully crafted films emerged from the new company.

When Fairbanks and Pickford decided to unite themselves domestically, however, they created tension among their associates. For both were already married, and the scandal of a twin divorce could well have finished their careers.

"Would the public accept them after that?" asked Adela Rogers St Johns. "Mary came to see me one day and said, 'You're a newspaper woman who's been in this a long time, and you're a judge of public opinion, and I want to ask you a question.' I can see her now. She was so tiny, that her feet didn't touch the floor. And all of a sudden she just leaned forward and with tears in her eyes, she said, 'Adela, if I divorce Owen and marry Douglas Fairbanks, will my people ever forgive me?'

"And she meant just that—'will my people ever forgive me?'— like a queen. And it was a hard question to answer, because in those days we did not regard divorce as just another game that you played before breakfast. I said, 'I believe—and I can only tell you what I

believe—that they will forgive you anything.'"

The divorces, which cost both Pickford and Fairbanks enormous sums, were engineered with discretion, and the aristocrats of Hollywood were permitted to become the industry's reigning monarchs. They indulged in a European tour. "They landed in Southampton," said Lord Mountbatten, "and England went absolutely mad about them. You see, we'd seen their films, and it was the first time people had a chance of seeing and hearing in real life people they had only seen in silent films before. They were fêted in a very big way."

Even in Moscow, a crowd of 300,000 turned out to watch their arrival at the station—for American features made up eighty per cent of the films the Russians saw. The Soviets even made their own Mary Pickford picture, by incorporating shots of Mary Pickford taken during the tour with a story of a cinema usher who imagines he's Douglas Fairbanks. One scene brings them together— and Mary Pickford obligingly throws her arms round the comedian and kisses him. The rest of the film shows the comic pursued by film-crazy Russians, determined to tear strips from his clothes as souvenirs. Satire it may have been, but *A Kiss from Mary Pickford* represented the most graphic possible comment on the success of the American star system.

The new combine proved beyond a shadow of a doubt that the public made the stars. The producers might offer a menu, but the public selected the dish. Every industry was dependent upon the consumer, but no industry, not even the world of fashion, was so slavishly dependent upon the whim of consumer as the motion picture. No matter how brilliant the story, how vast the sets, the only thing that mattered to the public was 'who's in it?' Said pioneer director Sidney Franklin: "You could take 1,000 feet of Norma Talmadge in a chair, and her fans would flock to see it."

Once the star system was set in motion, it shaped the industry as the slow, but irrevocable force of a glacier shaped a landscape. Virtually every advance in technique, every important development, could be attributed to it, from the close-up to the introduction of the feature film. Every ounce of creative energy was harnessed to bring the star closer in every sense to the audience.

Fashion was at first slavishly followed by moving pictures, but soon the star system demanded the importation of fashion designers, hairdressers, make-up artists—and by the 1920s, pictures set the fashion throughout the western world. Auxiliary industries fanned out around the studios, as towns spread around castles.

A side-effect of stardom was the permanent loss of the casual democracy of Hollywood, and the establishment of an aristocracy. "At the time of their reign in Pickfair," said Lord Mountbatten, "Mary Pickford and Douglas Fairbanks were treated like royalty, and in fact they behaved in the same sort of dignified way that royalty did. They also filled the role of running the very loose sort of society there would have been in Hollywood in those days. They were a great unifying force and, I think, a great force for the good."

They set standards which other stars felt they ought to emulate.

"I was married to Bebe Daniels," said Ben Lyon, "and she wanted to give a dinner party for Cecil B. DeMille. I bought some beautiful lilies and put them in the crystal bowl in the centre of the table.

We had the extra butler with the frock coat. The guests arrived, they had their drinks and we went down to the table. First thing, to my surprise, the water lilies closed up, because they closed at night—I didn't realise that. They looked like artichokes. Then we had a lovely dinner. Little did we know that the butler had been drinking our liquor. He was stinking. He came in with a tray of sweets and he passed Mr DeMille. 'No, thank you,' said Mr DeMille. 'Oh, go on, sweetheart, have some. They're lovely,' and he slid the tray across his bald head. Well, I didn't work for DeMille after that."

Gloria Swanson was the first Hollywood star to marry an authentic title—actually, the Marquis Henri de la Falaise de la Coudraye. He was known as 'Hank' in Hollywood; Gloria Swanson had met him while she was making a picture in France. During the production, she had been seriously ill and nearly died. So that, coupled with her marriage, had aroused immense curiosity. Her return to California was epic; vast crowds met her with a hail of flowers, everyone in Hollywood turned out to greet her, and there was not just one band but two. Describing her return, Gloria Swanson said: "I hadn't been back to California for almost four years. We went down to the Grauman Theatre on Third Street, in Los Angeles. Now, there was a tunnel on Third Street and the traffic was pretty heavy, and we got trapped in it. I have a fit if I'm late. I'm a nervous wreck. It doesn't matter if it's an appointment with a garbage man. Now here I'm going to make a late entrance at my own opening . . . stuck in this tunnel and breathing all that awful gasoline.

"By the time we come out of the tunnel, there are people on top of the car, on the hood, on the runways, so that the chauffeur can hardly see where he's going. Finally we arrive at the theatre. We get out of the car, one behind the other, like Indians, and there's no one in the lobby and I say, 'You see, I'm late. Oh, isn't this terrible!' We walk in, get to the top of the aisle, the lights go on and the audience rise, turn around and sing 'Home Sweet Home' to me. This sounds corny now, but in 1925, with everybody who's in the business—somebody on crutches, I think it was Ernest Torrence, somebody else in a wheelchair—I just stood there and cried. I was escorted down the aisle with my husband and my mother behind me and I was placed between Cecil B. DeMille and Mack Sennett.

"After the film had been on about half an hour, somebody said we would have to get out by a side exit because the police couldn't handle the crowd that had gathered out front. So we crawled out. During the ride to Beverly Hills, I sat with my mother on one side and Henri on the other, and Henri said, 'Why are you so silent, Gloria? This should have been the greatest moment of your life.'

"And I said, 'Oh, you darlings don't understand. Everything you've seen tonight was not for my work as an artist. It was for a personality who came back—like Lazarus—from the dead, Cinderella who married the prince, and the Prodigal who's returned. That's the reason for the excitement. If I were to make the greatest picture of my whole career, that would never happen again. Now I have a problem. I have to go down the other side.'

"So I was on the rocky top of the precipice for several years . . . and then my career just went downhill."

BIOGRAPH COMPANY

ELEVEN EAST FOURTEENTH STREET

NEW YORK, N.Y.

May 21, 1910

Miss Betty Blayne,
    San Francisco, Calif.

Dear Madam:

        Replying to your letter of May 16th, we regret to state that we are not issuing photographs of the artists comprising our stock company. We are therefore returning your check for $2.50 enclosed with your letter.

            Yours very truly,

            BIOGRAPH COMPANY
L. E. W. — D.   L. E. W.
Enc.

The star image was manufactured and purveyed by the publicity machine. "We went along with it," said Buddy Rogers. "It was all part of Hollywood all part of our business. It was all a make-believe business at that time."

Stars were expected to hire their own press agents; in addition, studio press agents bombarded the newspapers and magazines with stories.

"I don't know of any publicity that was truthful in those days," said Irving Asher. "I was the first press agent for Warner Brothers studios, and I knew no more about it than you know how to fly a Jumbo jet. But anything I wrote and sent to the papers, they'd print. They'd print anything to do with movie stars. Ninety per cent of it was manufactured. You read tales of marble being imported from Italy for some movie star's bathroom . . . Everyone made a million dollars a minute, and had six Rolls-Royces and every picture cost a million dollars. Few pictures in those days cost a million. A picture cost a hundred, two hundred thousand dollars, and that was a big super production."

The star system supported not only the film industry, but investors from the garment trade, the cosmetic business, the furniture industry and countless other enterprises, whose products received lavish commercials from Hollywood in virtually every release. These interests held a powerful grip on Hollywood, but no stranglehold was tighter than that of the stars. Their despotic powers aroused the antagonism of the producers, who felt responsible for their success, and towards the end of the silent era the big stars had their wings clipped and were brought down to earth. Their kingdom was usurped by the producers, and ironclad contracts discouraged them from taking off and overshadowing the picture business again.

left] The stars of the Biograph films were anonymous— far from attempting to foster their popularity among fans, the company discouraged all signs of interest.

While flat lighting had been acceptable in the early years, Cecil B. DeMille's cameraman, Alvin Wyckoff, instituted Rembrandt lighting around 1915. Blanche Sweet had played the title role in *Judith of Bethulia* (1913) for Griffith, and had been one of the anonymous young players at Biograph. She moved to the Lasky Feature Play Company, and got more money, better production values, star billing and Rembrandt lighting—but she still found it all an anti-climax after Griffith. A scene from *The Warrens of Virginia* (1915) a Civil War story which, with DeMille's characteristic good fortune, came out a week after *The Birth of a Nation* première. Like the Griffith film, it drew on family experience, in this case the adventures of DeMille's grandfather.

W68

By 1914, the star system was beginning to triumph. Producers felt that if they didn't have a star, they didn't have a hope. It would be unfair to call Theda Bara an entirely manufactured star, because she had a quality unique on the screen. She played a vamp—the first purely erotic woman in pictures. She was given a totally new persona by press agents at Fox; like Barnum, they had firm faith in public gullibility, and they made up some extraordinary stories. Theda Bara was an anagram of 'Arab Death' . . . born in the shadow of the Sphinx . . . all that sort of nonsense; her real name was Theodosia Goodman. She had a strong sense of humour, went along with it all and for three years, made enormous sums of money for

Fox, ranking third behind Pickford and Chaplin. But as the picture on the right suggests, the Fox people weren't quite sure which direction their character might go. They put her in 'good woman' parts, such as *Heart and Soul*, which were disliked; it was downhill, thereafter, in every picture. (Below, *Cleopatra*, 1917.)

On the screen, Theda was obnoxious. She was arrogant, rude to servants and delightfully detestable, as any woman who conveyed unbridled eroticism had to be seen to be. The vampire cycle was short lived, and by the end of World War One, Theda's day was over. In the 'twenties, she parodied her old roles for Hal Roach, in two-reel comedies.

left] The great opera star Geraldine Farrar (left) in the title role of *Carmen* (1915), directed by Cecil B. DeMille. With her is another important figure, Jeanie Macpherson, an actress who became Cecil B. DeMille's star writer.

The most successful star of the entire silent era—not even Chaplin exceeded her for popularity—Mary Pickford attained that position with a series of delightful pictures, made with care and skill, *Daddy Long Legs* (1919) directed by Marshall Neilan, was among her best. yet has been completely forgotten today, as have so many of her others. Mary Pickford's exacting standards dismayed her directors; she was constantly critical of her own performance and insisted on retakes. But she enhanced the reputation of almost every director she worked with.

above] Douglas Fairbanks, and his wife Mary Pickford, were the two most consistently popular stars of the silent era. Representing Hollywood royalty, they held court at their mansion, Pickfair, and received regal acclaim when they toured the world—the crowds jamming the streets as enthusiastically in Moscow as in London and Paris. They made it their job to understand every facet of production and controlled their own pictures. Although neither of them directed, both were quite capable of doing so. Making pictures for them was a game, which had to be made more complex, more adventurous to keep up the fun . . . larger sets, more lavish special effects, wilder stunts. They took their work seriously, but they enjoyed it as much as the audience, and their pictures were immensely successful. Here they pose at the entrance to their newly-acquired ten acre studio, at 7200 Santa Monica Boulevard, where some of the finest films of the silent era would be produced: February, 1922. (The odd thing is that the sign is the wrong way round—that's Santa Monica Boulevard behind the gate—so the sign must have been painted just for this publicity picture.)

left] Douglas Fairbanks spent extravagantly on all his costume pictures, to the despair of his brother John, who had charge of finances. "These things have to be done properly," Doug would say, "or not at all." He was triumphantly vindicated by the result. A scene from *The Thief of Bagdad* (1924), directed by Raoul Walsh.

Douglas Fairbanks was initially alarmed by the immensity of these
sets for *Robin Hood* (1922). He had ordered them, but when
confronted by the vast castle walls, felt that his character would be
swamped by the sheer size. Director Allan Dwan won him over, and
Robin Hood became one of Fairbanks's best pictures. The scale of
the castle, incidentally, exceeds even the city of Babylon built for
Intolerance. The street in the foreground is Santa Monica Boulevard,
complete with the streetcar and railroad tracks which, until
recently, ran down the centre.

Influenced by the German fantasy films he had seen on his trip abroad, Fairbanks outdid *Robin Hood* for grandeur with *The Thief of Bagdad* (1924). The sets were designed by William Cameron Menzies, a brilliant art director (best remembered for his film *Things to Come*). Fairbanks flew over this set on a magic carpet—suspended by wires from a gigantic crane. Part of the *Robin Hood* castle can be glimpsed at top right.

Gloria Swanson began her career as a comedienne—here she is
in 1917 at Mack Sennett with Juanita Hansen (right). She insists
she was not a successful one. "I played my comedies like Duse,"
she says, "which is probably why I was so funny." Her life changed
when she was signed by Cecil B. DeMille.

L.J.-102

Marion Davies was as much a 'manufactured' star as Theda Bara. Newspaper tycoon William Randolph Hearst sank enormous sums into her pictures—smothering her with vast sets—unnerving her with glittering casts from the New York stage—and he spent further enormous sums on exploitation. Poor Marion Davies! By all the rules she should have sunk under the weight of Hearst's expectations There was criticism of her 'utterly ridiculous' publicity, and *Picture Play* magazine remarked: "She should have retired years ago when it seemed clear she was definitely not going to catch on with the decisive film-going public." Hearst once admitted that none of her

pictures made money, but he used them for tax-deduction purposes.

Fortunately, Marion stuck it out, and when Hearst joined forces with Metro-Goldwyn-Mayer, Irving Thalberg recognised her true talent and starred her in a series of popular pictures which revealed her as a brilliant comedienne. The farewell scene (left) is from *Yolanda* (1924), the last of her medieval costume dramas, directed by Robert Vignola. The still above is from *Marianne* (1929) directed by Robert Z. Leonard, simultaneously her last silent and first talkie (it was released in both versions), which took advantage of her gift for mimicry.

Evans
L.A.

left] Colleen Moore, as she was at the beginning of her career in 1917. She became enormously popular in the 'twenties. A 1929 advertisement claimed, "For the third successive year, Colleen Moore leads the world in box office receipts." A brilliant light comedienne, she helped to popularise the flapper with films like *Flaming Youth* (1923).

"I was the spark that lit up 'Flaming Youth'," said F. Scott Fitzgerald, "and Colleen Moore was the torch. What little things we are to have caused that conflagration."

The stars imposed on the public may have been theatrical luminaries—but the stars chosen by the public often had no theatrical experience, and were pure movie stars. Norma Talmadge (above) was one of these. Her sister, Constance, was an excellent comedienne (another sister married Buster Keaton) but Norma specialised in emotional roles. She was a brilliant actress, and it is a tragedy that so few of her films are available today.

Q755·81

Two studies of Clara Bow, which convey something of the astonishing timelessness of her appeal. Yet she embodied to perfection the period in which she starred. "I thought she was the most marvellous star of the 'twenties," said Louise Brooks, "because she *was* the 'twenties. Garbo came from Europe, Swanson was already very sophisticated and dressy in DeMille films, but Clara was the real jazz baby."

Born in Brooklyn, Clara had the sort of deprived childhood that would have made a harrowing film; she had to cope with a mentally ill mother who tried several times to kill her. When little more than a child, she won a personality contest and appeared in Elmer Clifton's *Down to the Sea in Ships* (1922). She was signed to a long-term contract and put through the Poverty Row mill in Hollywood; in one year, she appeared in fifteen pictures. When her producer, B. P. Schulberg, took her to Paramount, her career blossomed and she made her best loved pictures. Her impact upon her generation cannot be over estimated.

Lillian Gish, at the time of *Way Down East* (1920). Her fragile beauty is apparent from this photograph, but you have to see such films as *Orphans of the Storm* and *The Wind* to appreciate her brilliance as an actress. She was able to convey intense emotion by little more than a quiver. D. W. Griffith trained Lillian, and her sister, Dorothy, an outstanding comedienne; in 1919, Lillian directed her sister in *Remodelling Her Husband*. Later, during the 'twenties, Lillian acted as producer of her own starring vehicles.

right] Photographs of Mary Astor by the great photographer Albin first aroused John Barrymore's interest in the young actress. Their screen partnership, in films like *Beau Brummel* (1924) and *Don Juan* (1926), was paralleled by an off-screen romance. Right, a scene from a proposed version of *Paola and Francesca*. "He taught me respect for acting," said Mary Astor. "He said, 'Do everything they give you—and do it right. Don't say, "Oh, well, it's nothing, and slough it through." Stick your nose in the air and do it the best you can.'"

Silent stars may have a reputation for tempestuous temperament, but they didn't always take themselves *that* seriously! Ramon Novarro (in costume for *A Certain Young Man*), John Gilbert (in costume for *Bardelys the Magnificent*) and Roy D'Arcy (in costume for *The Temptress*) pose for a gag shot at MGM, 1926.

CHAPTER SIXTEEN

Great Lover of the Silver Screen

Rudolph Valentino

RUDOLPH VALENTINO has had a raw deal from history. His acting style seems comic to modern eyes; his private life seems a sick joke, thanks to a film biography. And a stream of lurid paperbacks fills in the gaps.

Valentino's career *was* extraordinary. He *did* have difficulties in his private life. But he has been subjected to more slander and innuendo than virtually any other motion picture star. And all for one reason; he was the greatest lover of the silver screen.

Valentino was an elegant and polished actor, but there were plenty of elegant and polished actors in Hollywood. What aroused so much fascination was his effect on women in the audience. No other star in film history had such a shattering impact. And when it was whispered that he had problems with women in his private life, the poor man was doomed. You can play a Bluebeard without murdering your wives, but you can't play a Casanova, apparently, without being one.

Valentino's acting style has suffered. Whenever he is seen on television, extracts are selected that make him look ridiculous. And it's the same with photographs; publishers invariably choose those in which his eyes are popping with passion. Unfortunately, Valentino was not well served by his material. He made more poor films in his short career than good ones. Most of them were romantic *kitsch*, as dated as the stories that inspired them. Yet how triumphantly his personality transcended such material!

Biographers try to link the earthy passions of his beginnings as an illiterate Italian peasant, sweating in the fields to eke out a living, with his love-making on the screen. Unfortunately, he wasn't an illiterate peasant.

"We were not a rich family," said his brother, Alberto, "neither were we an aristocratic one. We were in the middle class. My father was a veterinarian, a health officer and a biologist. There have been written stories—not truthful—that Rudy came to America because he was a poor boy, an immigrant, to make money. No. In his life, he was always pushed by the spirit of adventure. For him, America was the great nation, and he wanted to know it. So it was the spirit of adventure which brought him here. He was very proud, and in order not to worry my mother, when he wrote home he went to the Waldorf-Astoria and wrote letters from there. But he was not a guest of the Waldorf. On the contrary, he told me that sometimes he even slept in Central Park."

Valentino was an outstanding natural dancer, and he secured a job at a New York cafe, dancing with the customers. It was a common enough experience at the time, but it was to blight his chances when he came to Hollywood.

"It was a joy to dance with Valentino," said Viola Dana, "but my escort, Tony Moreno, said, 'Never do that. Never dance with Valentino.' I said, 'Why not?' He said, 'Don't you know he has a bad reputation?' 'No,' I said, 'I don't know anything about him.' 'Well,' he said, 'he has the reputation of being a gigolo.' 'What's that?' I said. 'He used to get paid for dancing with women.' 'I don't see anything wrong with that,' I said. 'I danced with him because he's a darn good dancer.'"

Valentino was still playing bit parts, and his reputation as a gigolo, coupled with rumours of his involvement in a divorce suit in New York, did not help his popularity. Viola Dana encountered him again one Christmas Eve. She discovered that he was on his own, with nowhere to go. "I was living with my sister and her husband. I said, 'You're going to come with me. This is our big night. My mother and father will be there, with presents, and you're going to be right with us.' He said, 'That'll be marvellous.' So we made him Santa Claus. We put a red cape and a red hat on him and we got cottonwool and put a beard on him, and he handed out the presents. He stayed over Christmas and I don't think he ever forgot it. It made me laugh—a lot of people said how well they knew Rudy, and what they did for him and I thought, 'Mmmm . . . there was one Christmas they forgot about Rudy, before he was anything.' After he did *The Four Horsemen* it was different."

The Four Horsemen of the Apocalypse, under the direction of Rex Ingram, brought Valentino to prominence. He had worked hard for it. Latin types had not been in vogue, and he had subsisted on a meagre diet of gangster parts, seducers and lounge lizards. Nevertheless, they were ideal training for the role of Julio Desnoyers, a new kind of leading man in an age of flawless heroes; the sleek, assured Latin lover, selfish, sensual, totally compelling. *The Sheik* caught the impact of *The Four Horsemen* and raised Valentino to the pinnacle of stardom.

Yet his private life was no mirror of his screen image. His first marriage to Jean Acker, a protégée of the Russian actress Nazimova, was a disaster, and his second, to another Nazimova discovery, led him to court on bigamy charges. Valentino had failed to comprehend that under Californian law, a full year was demanded between divorce and remarriage.

Valentino met his second wife, an American heiress called Winifred Hudnut, on the set of *Camille* (in which he played opposite Nazimova). She had changed her name, like most dancers of the period, to something suitably Russian, and as Natacha Rambova she was building herself an additional career as an art director.

Natacha, Rudy and cameraman Paul Ivano lived in a house on Sunset Boulevard while Jean Acker was trying to get proof that Rudy was unlawfully cohabitating in the State of California. During this potentially dangerous situation, Natacha asked Ivano to buy her a mountain lion cub. He did so, but they found the animal only took to Ivano, and insisted on sleeping on his bed. "Even little mountain lions get bigger," said Ivano, "and in a few months she

86-241

right] The fact that Rudolph Valentino played Latin lovers seems, to his detractors, to deprive him of all right to a sense of humour. Yet he could laugh at himself—as he did in *The Eagle* (1925)—and he knew just how far fetched his reputation was. Few of his films were intended to be realistic—*The Sheik* (1921), *Blood and Sand* (1922) and the rest were meant to be escapism, an exaggerated dream world, aimed at that most susceptible of audiences, the readers of romantic fiction.

Here, director Fred Niblo and Valentino clown about with an obliging donkey during the making of *Blood and Sand*.

below] Valentino has been characterised in print and on the screen with envious venom. But these 'biographers' never knew him, and their picture of a limp-wristed lounge lizard has never rung true. Here, in contrast, is another Valentino—the young man with an intense interest in machinery, loading his own 35 mm Debrie camera to make his personal record of *A Sainted Devil* (1924).

overwhelming telegram to his hotel so he'd be reassured that all I wanted to do in life was go to that opening with him.

"We sat through 'The Big Parade' and I cried and my handkerchief was torn to pieces—and his also. It was a very sad evening."

The reviews were unanimous raves. "No such adjectives had been used to describe a movie," wrote Gilbert. "I sat for hours crying and thrilling to the printed phrases. Then I staggered to bed and slept round the clock.

"I had sounded the depths and reached the peak of emotional excitement. I never expect such an experience to occur to me again. And so I say, and please understand, that I have concluded my career in pictures." Written in 1928, before he knew the reaction to his first sound film, the bravado behind those words strikes a chillingly ironic note.

Gilbert's fame reached legendary proportions when the name of another star was linked romantically with his. "I had already started a picture," said Clarence Brown, "and we were trying to get a woman to play opposite John Gilbert. We were up at Arrowhead on our first locations when the studio gave us the okay to go ahead with Greta Garbo. And it just happened that the scenes we started shooting when we got back were the scenes in which Garbo was introduced to Gilbert at the railroad station. From then on, that was the development of their love affair in the picture. I just had a real love affair going for me that you couldn't beat any way you tried."

"It was an explosion," said Adela Rogers St Johns. "They looked at each other and said all those awful, trite things that we don't say any more. 'Where have you been all my life?' and 'You are everything.' I have never seen two people so violently, excitedly in love. I mean, when she walked through a door—if he was in the room—he went white and took a great long breath and then walked toward her as though he were being yanked by a magnet or something. She had always been rather aloof, but she just adored him, and when they made love scenes together for a movie they had sometimes to be censored a little bit. They were so violently in love they couldn't conceal it."

"She's hard to classify," said Eleanor Boardman. "Because, like Chaplin, she was man, women and child. You can't pigeon-hole Garbo. She was fascinating. Extremely selfish, beautiful, strange. She'd walk around Jack Gilbert's garden perfectly nude, with a dressing gown over her back. She was completely unconscious, being a Swede, and was quite used to it. She was an introvert, but adorable."

Gilbert proposed to Garbo, and she accepted. At the same time, Vidor planned to marry Eleanor Boardman, and they agreed to make it a double wedding. The ceremony was attended by Louis B. Mayer. Garbo failed to appear. "Gilbert was getting very nervous," said Eleanor Boardman, "he was getting rather violent. It seems that Mayer was in the men's room with Gilbert and Gilbert was crying about this situation, and Mayer said, 'Sleep with her, don't marry her.' Gilbert socked him, and knocked him down and he hit his head on a tile. And that was really the beginning of the end of Gilbert's career."

"After Jack had knocked him down," said his daughter Leatrice

Gilbert Fountain, "and drawn blood, Mayer said, 'I'll destroy you.' From that point on you can see Jack's career going like this; he is pulling in one direction, and some absolute force is pulling him back."

In 1928, Jack Gilbert signed a contract which made him incredibly wealthy and, as he thought, kept him away from the vindictiveness of Mayer. It ensured that his pictures would be supervised by Thalberg, and the contract had the built-in protection of Nicholas Schenck. Schenck had succeeded Marcus Loew as the power-behind-the-throne at MGM, and he conducted his own private feud with Mayer. Gilbert's contract, at the staggering fee of $1,500,000, represented a severe blow to Mayer's prestige, and it was not an act he could forgive.

By this time, sound was a certainty and all the studios were going over to it, or going out of business. Gilbert's new contract made no provision for a voice test. He gave a public dress-rehearsal in *Hollywood Revue of 1929*, when he played the balcony scene from *Romeo and Juliet* opposite Norma Shearer. There were no complaints from the public, although one review referred to his speech being "too mincing and affected for words". Fortunately, the scene was also played in slang, and the burlesque wiped out the bad impression.

Gilbert had already finished his first sound film when he played this scene. His director was veteran actor Lionel Barrymore (who appeared in the same *Hollywood Revue* as the director). The film was given the risible title of *His Glorious Night*.

When audiences saw and heard Gilbert in a serious love scene, they killed his career with laughter. "It was the problem of an image," said King Vidor. 'Valentino had the same image, and I think he would have suffered the same death had he lived. You couldn't put this image into words. If you do, it becomes funny. People are waiting; what was he saying all the time in silent films? They hear him speak and all he says is, 'I love you, I love you, I love you.' They hear these words and laugh."

The idea that Gilbert had a squeaky voice has persisted for years. One theory suggests he was sabotaged by bad recording. We ran *His Glorious Night* for the series, and Gilbert's voice sounded no different to the other talkies in which he appears. It was quite low. The television technicians who saw it with us said he could not have been incorrectly recorded without affecting the other players in the same scene.

The direction, however, was lamentable. Gilbert seemed tense and his eyes constantly stared at the girl during the love scenes. The script was appalling, and worse still was Gilbert's delivery. His enunciation of every line with the correct 'pear-shaped' tones was what aroused the laughter. If only he had been encouraged to relax, and to abandon that dreadful enunciation. . .!

Said Variety: 'The dialogue is inane. Gilbert's prowess at love-making takes on a comedy aspect that gets them tittering at first, then laughing outright at the very first ring of the couple of dozen 'I love you' phrases designed to climax the thrill in the Gilbert lines.'

Recalling his foolhardiness with the Brulatour contract, he

refused to walk out of the MGM one. He sat it out, subjected to one poor picture after another, his box-office grosses falling as fast as shares on Wall Street, that desperate autumn of 1929.

Gilbert wanted to avoid any possibility of MGM dropping him for breach of contract, so he religiously attended the studio every day—even when there was no work. Some people were entrusted to make it difficult for him—the gateman sometimes failed to recognise him. There were other attempts at humiliation, aimed at forcing him to quit. But he wouldn't—even though he and Mayer were no longer on speaking terms. Not surprisingly, Gilbert began drinking very heavily. And at last, his contract expired.

Less than a year later, to their intense chagrin, MGM was forced to take Gilbert back again. Greta Garbo insisted on his playing the lead in the 1933 *Queen Christina*. Her motives can only be guessed at; they suggest a generosity rare in the film industry. At first she approved Laurence Olivier, but then she changed her mind. She evidently wanted to do something positive to help her old friend, who had once done so much to help her. It was an outstandingly brave decision, and thanks to director Rouben Mamoulian, it also proved a successful one.

JACK C. GILBERT
Staff Author
PARALTA PLAYS
Hollywood

Sadly, the success of *Queen Christina* did little to help Gilbert reconstruct his self-confidence. His last picture was a story in which he played a character the public now strongly suspected him to be—a dissipated, bitter, cynical drunk. In *The Captain Hates the Sea* (directed by Lewis Milestone for Columbia), Gilbert played an ex-Hollywood writer, pushing himself out on a cruise in the hopes of staying off the bottle and starting a new book.

"I think Gilbert was his own most destructive enemy," said Sam Marx. "He did not agree that his voice was wrong for his character. He took to drinking very heavily, and he sort of willed himself to die, in a beautiful place in Beverly Hills, surrounded by some rather attractive women and a lot of empty bottles."

The career of John Gilbert indicates that the star, and the person playing the star, were regarded by producers as separate entities, subject to totally different attitudes. Gilbert, as an ordinary human being, had no legal right to the stardom which was the sole property of the studio. When Gilbert, as an employee, tried to seize control of the future of Gilbert the star, the studio decided that to save their investment from falling into the hands of rivals, they had to wreck their property. Other properties—books, films, sets—were equally ephemeral, and although they had consumed vast amounts of effort, could be destroyed with impunity. But the destruction of a star carried with it the destruction of a person. Producers like Mayer behaved like scrap-yard proprietors, wrecking cars with the drivers still at the wheel. The star system undeniably brought pleasure to millions but it seems somehow abhorrent that it took such tragedies as that of John Gilbert to bring us our entertainment.

left] An almost unrecognisably young John Gilbert—an advertisement which, like Valentino's, comes from the 1918 Studio Directory. Gilbert was as fascinated by the technical side of movie making as by the acting side, and his ambition was to become a director.

right] Following *The Big Parade*, Gilbert was cast opposite Lillian Gish in *La Bohème* (1926), directed by King Vidor. Lillian Gish was anxious to try an experiment with the love scenes—playing them without physical contact. She wanted to show the lovers separated by a pane of glass, for instance, never actually touching until the final scene, which would then gain immense power from the accumulated tension. It was a good idea, but the front office decisively rejected it and ordered the love scenes taken over again.

423-119

CHAPTER EIGHTEEN

The Fellow who can't do Anything Else

The Director

THE early films were simple affairs, turned out rapidly to feed the ever-increasing demand from the growing ranks of exhibitors. Nothing much was required of the director but the ability to get the film out in time. The job was so simple that sometimes the cameraman could do it on his own. "In the beginning," said Allan Dwan, "there weren't any good directors, and there weren't any bad directors. It was a question of 'What's a director?' And the general answer was: 'He's the fellow who can't do anything else.'"

And yet the aura surrounding the role of director assumed an exalted radiance surprisingly early. The first directors, pensioned-off stage directors or unsuccessful actors, made up for the years wasted in the theatre with a grand show of omnipotence. In 1913, *Moving Picture World* was already talking about 'the early days', when the director was looked upon with the awe with which the Israelites regarded the golden calf: "The director was seen in the light of a tamer of wild animals. He was the man who could make the beasts go through their paces. All standards of dramatic art, and indeed all common sense, were flung to the winds. The director demanded that an altar be erected where incense was burned in his honour by day and by night. When we think of some of the directors who were then all-powerful, it sends a thrill through us to realise that the industry has survived them and that their gospel of cheapness and coarseness is out of date."

These words seem strange to us, because the films of the period have mostly vanished and the names of the first directors have been forgotten. A new generation of young and energetic directors swept the cynical older men out of the business; those who thought of "the fools that went to see moving pictures" and turned out rubbish, found themselves being directed in bit parts by men who had once formed part of that audience, men who loved the medium and were confident they could do better themselves.

One of these was Marshall 'Mickey' Neilan. Colleen Moore said of him: "I think he was one of our great directors, and they're going to discover him soon, if they can find his pictures. He was very inventive, and he had a marvellous sense of comedy. He did several of the very best Mary Pickfords. In those days, you didn't have a script. You just had a little outline. Marshall was able to invent as he went along. I think he was a genius."

The man responsible for giving Neilan his first break was Allan Dwan. "Neilan had worked for Griffith," said Dwan, "when he was a chauffeur. He'd carried people in and out of the studio, and he'd watched them work and on one or two occasions, he'd stepped into the crowd and was one of them. What I noticed about Neilan particularly were his good looks: he was a very handsome young fellow. He was also very talented; he had a remarkable sense for music, he was a good composer, and he had the typical Irish imagination one needs to have for that kind of personality." Neilan

began as an actor, and although he quickly graduated to directing, he continued to act.

Blanche Sweet was married to Neilan: "He had a way of telling a story and making a mere trifle seem twice as funny as it actually was," she said. "He could wrap Mary Pickford around his finger. He would disappear sometimes, and maybe wouldn't come in for a couple of hours, but let me tell you something; when he got to work, he made up for the lost time. If he didn't come to work, it was probably because he wasn't satisfied with the ideas that he had for it."

Neilan typified the flamboyant silent-film director; with seemingly inexhaustible energy, he would work all day and hold parties all evening. When the orchestra at the Coconut Grove finished for the night, he would invite them and the guests to his home and keep the party going until dawn. His early films were outstanding; he created an independent company, Marshall Neilan Productions, and could have become one of the most consistently successful box-office directors. But he was self-destructive. He drank a lot, affected a sort of Cohens-and-Kellys anti-Semitism which estranged him from the immigrant producers, and his pictures became less and less individual.

"Irving Thalberg was a very good friend of Marshall's, but Louis B. Mayer was, I think, a pre-natal enemy," said Blanche Sweet, "because it started in the womb, they hated each other so. We had our own unit at Goldwyn, and nobody else was allowed to interfere with our film in any way. We were on location in England for *Tess of the D'Urbervilles* when news of the Metro-Goldwyn merger reached us." Neilan made a few more films to wind up his contract, and left the company—tossing a lawsuit at Mayer for good measure.

"I guess," said Adela Rogers St Johns, "being ninety-two per cent Irish myself, I can say that what happened to Mickey Neilan was that he was Irish. You have to watch the Irish, you have to give them discipline, you have to have them in control of some kind. They can do the most brilliant things of anybody—which Mickey could—but he couldn't restrain his tongue. 'I was coming out of the Alexandria Bar one afternoon,' he said, 'and an empty taxicab drove up and Louis B. Mayer got out.' Well, we thought it was very funny. But Mayer didn't." Neilan was finished as a front-rank director by the mid-'twenties, yet he was active in the industry until the 1950s, when he played his last role in *A Face in the Crowd*.

Rex Ingram was another young Irishman who rapidly established such independence that he was allowed to leave Hollywood and operate from his own studio in the South of France. He, too, cultivated a deep loathing for Louis B. Mayer, which proved fatal for his career. "I would rank Ingram as number one director," said Byron Haskin. "Number one in the business. He was certainly way beyond Griffith, who was very crude and technically doesn't hold up at all. But Ingram's work forecast the coming of finesse in the movies. He had traces of sophistication that were not seen in films. Films had a child-like, fairy-tale quality. They were made to entertain, and that's that, but Ingram got into them nuances and values—I don't know any other director who reached that deeply."

Although few historians would agree with Haskin, Ingram was a great pictorialist; everything in his pictures was subordinate to the image. Collaborating with a brilliant editor, Grant Whytock, and a cameraman of genius, John Seitz, he created some of the most beautiful films of the entire silent era. He made a star of Valentino, with *The Four Horsemen*, and when Valentino left the company he took an extra from the crowd and created another star with Ramon Novarro. But Ingram was out of his time. He wanted to make what would now be called 'art films'—he followed *The Four Horsemen* with a jewel-like adaptation of Balzac's *Eugénie Grandet*, which he called *The Conquering Power*. It was not intended to duplicate the success of *The Four Horsemen*, nor did it. But he made too many unusual and offbeat films compared to popular successes. Ingram was greatly admired by other directors—Erich von Stroheim called him 'the world's greatest director'. Unfortunately, Ingram's dislike of Louis B. Mayer put him in a difficult position; Mayer laid his personal feelings aside so long as he produced box-office successes. When Ingram failed to do this with the bizarre and fascinating pictures he made in his own studios in the South of France, he found his independence quickly eroding. After one sound film, *Baroud*, he quit the business.

The producers controlled the business by the end of the silent era, and even the autocratic Cecil B. DeMille found his independence undermined. Having left Paramount, and formed his own studio, he was briefly obliged to work for Louis B. Mayer at MGM during the early days of sound.

DeMille had come into the business comparatively late for a pioneer—1913. He was, like Griffith, an actor and playwright. Of Griffith, DeMille said, "He was the teacher of us all," but DeMille owed a far greater debt to theatrical impresario David Belasco, for whom he and his brother William had worked. DeMille carried the Belasco style into pictures. "He wore puttees, and thumped around doing very extravagant things," said Adela Rogers St Johns, "and he had an office that was like a cathedral—it had stained glass windows around it. When you got in there, you were hypnotised by Mr DeMille. How did he see himself? Well, I think he gave God top place, but right under that there was Mr DeMille."

"The office was modelled after Belasco's, I believe," said his niece, Agnes de Mille. "You see, Cecil worked for him as a young man. and Belasco stole a play of his called *The Return of Peter Grimm*. I think Cecil's revenge was just to take the entire image out to Hollywood and do it better out there. His office had vaulted beams like a church, bear rugs on the floor, and light that was fixed on . . . the victim I was going to say . . . the interviewee, making him very uncomfortable, while the mastermind sat back in the shadows and studied what was going on."

DeMille was an outstanding director. He made some brilliant pictures in his early days, displaying a flair for action scenes that was equal to Griffith's. Only when he submitted completely to the whims of the exhibitors did his work begin to suffer. With typical irony, his worst picture, *The Ten Commandments* (1923), was his biggest success to date. His brilliant psychological dramas, like *Whispering Chorus* (1917) were too morbid for the popular taste. Immersed in his society dramas and Biblical epics, he seemed to change personality. It was as though a totally different director made those films, compared to the young man who came to Hollywood in 1913 and displayed such a keen sense of cinema. By the mid-'twenties, DeMille was a synonym for vast beds, sunken bathrooms and barbaric orgies.

"I think he was filming his own daydreams," said Agnes de Mille. "He was very young in some ways. I think Cecil really found all these things extraordinarily lovely. He really did like voluptuous young women. He really did like them all rolling around in his bed. He had been raised differently, he'd come from quite a different background. He didn't have it himself, but I think he dallied in the thoughts of it, and considered it enormously attractive."

"He was the king," said Henry Hathaway. "I only worked for him on a couple of pictures, but I could see that he ran the studio, he was the one that made all the money. He was an autocrat. But I guess he deserved to be. Everybody was trained when they worked with him. Anne Bauchens was the script girl and editor, and he always had a little megaphone. He'd just let go of it, and if Anne wasn't there to catch it, it would fall on the floor and she would get hell. He'd never look. He'd just let it go. There was a guy that just followed him with a chair. That was me. And when he sat down, that chair better be there.

"He had such discipline on the set. When we were working on *The Ten Commandments* they had a scene at the ocean. He was looking for a shot, and he walked towards the water. All his people, and there were about eight of them, walked right in with him, up to the waist in water. They had not a damn thing to do with finding the shot—he was just looking—but they all felt he might put out his hand and they'd better be there."

*　　*　　*

The American directors of the silent era were invariably young, and the most successful remained active for several decades, forming the backbone of the picture business. Some of the most respected directors of film history—Henry King, John Ford, King Vidor, Clarence Brown—are known for their classic sound films. But it was the silent studios that gave them their start, their training . . . and it was in their silent films that they first established their fascination with their American background.

"I went back to my home in Galveston, Texas, last year," said King Vidor, "and went into the house where I was born, went up the stairs, and looked down—and there was the stairway from *The Crowd*, the door and the automobile out in front at the curb. I'm sure that the idea of the young boy having to climb the stairs to the room where his father lay dying—I'm sure that came out of my childhood.

"I told Thalberg, 'This may not pack the theatres as much as we hope, I can't tell.' And he said, 'Well, I think MGM is making enough money that they can afford an experimental film every once in a while. It'll do something for the studio, and it will do something for the whole industry.' So that was a pretty good attitude for a top production executive!"

The Crowd (1928) has become famous as an outstanding film of the social conditions in America just before the Wall Street crash. It describes the hopes of an ordinary young man, and shows them slowly slipping away as he settles into the humdrum reality of family life. A deeply moving film, it was eloquently played by James Murray and Eleanor Boardman (the then Mrs King Vidor).

"I had a pretty clear picture of what the man should look like," said Vidor, "and I'd been looking around various places. One day I was talking to someone and a bunch of extras was going by. This fellow stopped and jumped between us—did a little dance—and I knew that he was the fellow I'd been looking for. I followed him, got his name and asked him to come to the studio. He didn't show up for about two days, so I had to go back and look at all the names of the extras working that day, remembering the one he told me, and we called him and paid him for a day's work to come out for an interview. We made a test—and he was miraculous."

"I didn't care about ordinary people," said Eleanor Boardman. "I thought when you went into movies that you wore pearls and beautiful hats, and gorgeous clothes . . . Suddenly I was cast in this downtrodden story, and I didn't like to be so drab and unattractive. I made no objection about it, however. I had confidence in Vidor."

Vidor had such a remarkable rapport with his players that it was seldom necessary for him to articulate what he needed. He was so much a part of their own emotions, that some players were hardly aware of his contribution. "You never got a great deal of direction from Vidor," said Eleanor Boardman. "He was a Christian Scientist, and he felt that people had cast themselves. If you're right for the part, you'll get it. I believe that too."

In one of the most difficult scenes, Eleanor Boardman had to take part in a domestic tiff, then, when her husband left, had to convey the fact that she was pregnant—she had forgotten to tell him. The result was a triumph of directing and acting.

"It was the first scene in the picture, at nine o'clock in the morning, when you don't feel particularly dramatic. You have to warm up to things like that. But we set it, with the camera and lights, we played it through, Vidor said, 'We'll take it once again,' when I really got into it, and that was it. I was lucky, and I was so happy it was over with."

MGM was attuned to glamour pictures and happy endings, and no one knew how to end *The Crowd*.

"We made seven endings," said Vidor, "and finally I came up with the ending where he's lost again in the crowd—the camera moves back, back, with a multiple series of images. Still they didn't want to buy that semi-cynical ending, and they made me send the picture out with a happy ending also. The exhibitor had the right

The first directors were former stage men with little understanding of the new medium. They were nearly all swept away by a new generation. Here, Fred Wright directs *Power* (1916) for Essanay of Chicago at Starved Rock, Illinois. The girl is Nell Craig. The cameraman operates one of the original 1912 model Bell and Howells.

to choose one or the other, but I never heard of the happy ending being shown anyplace. It was so false; the young couple had become prosperous and we see them at Christmas in a wealthy home. It was so ridiculous that I'm sure no exhibitor with an ounce of intelligence would ever run it, but it was there—he could run it if he thought the other was too downbeat."

It is a tribute to the moviegoers of the time that *The Crowd* was not cold-shouldered, but warmly welcomed. It was no smash hit, but it returned a modest profit to the studio. Unfortunately, the silent era was over by the time it was finished, and instead of being the first of a series of offbeat social pictures, it remained unique.

below] Lloyd Bacon was also a former stage man, but the younger men were more attuned to the potential of the medium, and made better film directors. Here he directs Monte Blue in a Warner Brothers film, *No Defense* (1929), one of the last silents, which was released with a few talking sequences. (Bacon was later responsible for such classics as *42nd Street*.) The breeches and boots were regulation wear for silent film directors, not only for their air of authority—they made them look like officers in the army—but because life on location demanded such protection. The hat, with the title of the film on the front, was evidently Bacon's idea. I wish I knew what was written on the back . . . .

left] One could make a broad generalisation about Hollywood in the silent days, and say that if the business side of the industry was run by Jews, the creative side was the domain of the Irish. Here we have that uneasy combination graphically presented, and it takes a girl from Brooklyn with Scots blood (Anita Stewart) to hold them together. Louis B. Mayer (left) and Marshall Neilan (right) were 'pre-natal enemies' according to Neilan's wife, Blanche Sweet. Hardly was this film, *In Old Kentucky* (1919), into production when Neilan and Mayer began battling. Neilan resented Mayer's presence on location According to Jack Spears, "Neilan scalded Mayer with the sarcastic venom reserved for the 'money men' he so thoroughly despised. Mayer had a tough hide, but he did not forget. . . ." It was rare for a producer to come on location, for in those days the director was the whole show, and the producer had no role in the shooting. Front office interference, and the supervisor system, came later . . . largely thanks to the gentleman on the left. (On the parallel at right is cameraman Henry Cronjager.)

above] Cecil Blount DeMille, like most American directors, had been an actor—and he remained an actor for the rest of his life. A clue to his flamboyant style—which came to represent the apotheosis of Hollywood—was provided by someone who used to meet DeMille at home. Away from the studio, he was, apparently, a surprisingly shy, quiet man. The swashbuckling façade, the puttees, the revolver, the acid remarks, were simply the disguise a shy man needed to get through the day.

DeMille's early years were the most rewarding, for his films, made with care and dedication, were often outstanding. At this period, he was, in many ways, a more sophisticated director than D. W. Griffith. Unfortunately, his favourite pictures were not the most commercial, and when he realised the kind of hokum that made money, he made it—bigger and brassier than anyone else. Here, he directs one of his best pictures, *Joan the Woman* (1917); his assistant rallies the troops with a bugle, and a violinist, instructed to follow him everywhere, provides background music for the scene.

209

MGM·6072

left] King Vidor (right of camera) prepares to shoot a Coney Island scene for *The Crowd* in January, 1927. Henry Sharp at camera; James Murray, grinning into the lens; Eleanor Boardman; and Bert Roach, top right. The camera is about to slide down ahead of the players.

above] *Tol'able David* (1921) is one of the enduring classics of the American screen. The story was written by Joseph Hergesheimer (centre), here seen visiting the location, Crabbottom (now Blue Grass), West Virginia, with Richard Barthelmess, the star (left) and director Henry King, who compares the book with the script. King was born eighty miles from the location, and infused the film with his own boyhood memories. D. W. Griffith is said to have prepared a treatment for the film, but since he seldom wrote scripts for anything, the idea is probably wishful thinking. For *Tol'able David* had all the strengths of a Griffith film without the drawbacks of exaggerated melodrama. One Griffith influence, however, is visible in the lower right-hand corner—the straw hat with the holes cut in it.

211

324-144

A film with roots in a director's childhood was *Man, Woman and Sin* (1927), written and directed for MGM by Monta Bell. One of the attractive aspects of the film was its casual depiction of life in the slums of Washington, D.C.; whites live next door to blacks without anyone making a fuss about it. The boy grows up to be a Washington reporter, just like Monta Bell. The film starred John Gilbert and Jeanne Eagels—and Gilbert contributed enormously to the richness of the picture. The second half had a great deal in common with a favourite project of his, *The Widow in the Bye Street*, a poem by John Masefield, which Louis B. Mayer had refused to let him do. Under the new title, however, he failed to recognise it.

left] "I went back to my home in Galveston, Texas," said King Vidor, "and went into the house where I was born, went up the stairs, and looked down—and there was the stairway from *The Crowd*, the door, and the automobile out in front at the curb. I'm sure that the idea of the young boy having to climb the stairs to the room where his father lay dying—I'm sure that came out of my childhood."

right] Rex Ingram (centre) was a great pictorialist whose enthusiasm centred entirely around silent films. (He made one talkie and quit the business.) He was aided by his brilliant cameraman, John Seitz. Here they pose for a production shot during the making of *The Prisoner of Zenda* (1922); Ramon Novarro (left) Johnny George (foreground).

Sidney Franklin, below trying to rescue his script during the production of *Unseen Forces* (1921), began as a director in 1914 in partnership with his brother Chester. They made some outstanding films for D. W. Griffith's Fine Arts Studio, and were then placed under contract by Fox, for whom they directed some lavish fairy tales, acted almost entirely by children. After the war, they directed independently. Chester made some good films, but never matched the success of Sidney, who went from strength to strength.

PUB-959

215

Lois Weber was the most outstanding woman director in the early silent days. One hardly needs the qualification 'woman', for the commitment and technical expertise she displayed puts her on a par with the best of the men. A former church missionary, she was concerned with social issues—birth control, racial prejudice, capital punishment. She married Phillips Smalley, and they wrote, directed and acted in their own films. But Miss Weber's talent outweighed that of her husband—"he did all the shouting", said someone who worked with them—and she was the dominant member of the team. She made some important pictures at Universal, and tried to launch her own independent company. The films were not commercially successful (although only one survives, *The Blot*, it is an excellent picture) and her career slumped dramatically.

Besides Lois Weber, there were a surprising number of women who tried directing in the silent days, but only Dorothy Arzner ever held her own commercially. A former editor—responsible for *Blood and Sand* and *The Covered Wagon*—she was on the point of leaving Paramount when the front office agreed to her becoming a director in 1927. Here she poses with cameraman Al Gilks on the set of *Get Your Man* (1927). Her megaphone doubles as a viewfinder; as the original caption remarked: "It took a woman to discover this one!"

Maurice Tourneur, with Shirley Mason, on the set of
Treasure Island (1920). Tourneur, who arrived in America in
1914, was a pioneer of pictorialism. With his great art director
Ben Carré, and his equally brilliant cameraman, John van den
Broek, he directed a group of pictures which, by their sheer
beauty, created new standards for the industry. Later masters of
the craft, like Rex Ingram and Josef von Sternberg, were
profoundly influenced by Tourneur. Sadly, films could not make
money by beauty alone, and Tourneur found he had to collaborate
with the exhibitors to survive. He was overtaken by his rivals, and
in 1926, returned to France, where he continued directing.
However, his assistant director, Clarence Brown, carried his ideals
forward in the films he made for Universal and MGM.
"Tourneur," said Brown, "was my god."

Clarence Brown and Pauline Frederick on the set of *Smouldering Fires* (1924). The greatest cultural tragedy of the picture business has been the wilful disinterest of the major companies in their past achievements. Various administrations of Universal managed to let slip virtually their entire silent output, aided by fires and chemical decomposition. As a result, hundreds of fascinating films like this one have been lost for ever. *Smouldering Fires* only survived because a historian, John Huntley, rescued it from Johannesburg, where the local Kodascope library retained a print on 16 mm. It proved to be a minor masterpiece, a study of the pressures on a woman of forty in charge of a factory. Pauline Frederick, a stage star who had her biggest success with *Madame X* (1920), played the lead brilliantly. The film won Clarence Brown a contract to direct Valentino, because a producer thought he was watching an Ernst Lubitsch film.

Silent film directors often found it hard to convey what they wanted with words. They thought in visual terms, and since most of them had been actors, they found demonstration easier than instruction. Here, Jack Conway shows an amused Miss Dupont how he wants her to read a letter. Elinor Hancock, right. *The Rage of Paris* (1921).

left] Reginald Barker was one of the unsung heroes of the early silent days—the director of some of the best of the Thomas Ince pictures. Unfortunately for Barker, Ince took credit for direction whenever he thought it would help the film commercially, and Barker's name has been forgotten. Nevertheless, Barker was at his best when surrounded by the excellent facilities of the Ince studios, and his career faded somewhat in the 'twenties.

Born in Canada, brought up in Scotland, Barker worked on the stage until he entered the picture business in 1913. For Ince, he made *The Coward* with Charles Ray, *Typhoon* and *Wrath of the Gods* with Sessue Hayakawa, *The Bargain* with William S. Hart and *The Italian* with George Beban. All these films survive, and represent some of the finest achievements of the early American cinema.

right] This will strike a chord with any film maker who sees it, for that screen-shaped gesture is still part of the film technician's sign language. Cameraman John Mescall, right, is talking to director Rupert Hughes (uncle of Howard) and assistant cameraman Charles Marshall on the 1924 Goldwyn production about Hollywood, *Souls for Sale*.

below] When the Paramount Astoria studios closed for a year, Frank Tuttle, a writer, Dwight Wiman, Osgood Perkins and cameraman Fred Waller formed themselves into the Film Guild, an equivalent of the Theatre Guild, with the intention of producing pictures which were artistic rather than commercial. The group made five films, and Tuttle directed all of them. Here Tuttle, left, and actor Glenn Hunter examine a scene from the Film Guild's first, *Cradle Buster* (1922). Tuttle rapidly became a top director (in the 'thirties, he made *Roman Scandals*). Fred Waller developed the process known as Cinerama. This is clearly a posed picture—no editor would allow the hot Klieg light so close to the highly inflammable film—and the hand-cranked viewing machine is a luxury. Most editors cut by hand. Come to think of it, where *is* the editor?

223

CHAPTER NINETEEN

When Hollywood Ruled the World

On Location Abroad

left] Henry King directing *Romola* (1924) on location in Italy. The medieval city of Florence would have been an ideal background for the George Eliot novel, were it not for the traffic and the streetcars that tended to get in the way. Henry King rented the Vise studio, Florence, and his art director, Robert Haas, rebuilt the ancient city with meticulous authenticity. The resulting film, which starred Lillian and Dorothy Gish, and Ronald Colman, was visually exquisite. Roy Overbaugh, leaning on the Bell and Howell camera, won much praise for his photography.

right, above] *Ben Hur* (1925) should have cured the Americans of making pictures in foreign lands. Italy was swept by political dissension—Mussolini was in power, and socialist fought fascist at every opportunity—and the picture was dogged by delay. The first director, Charles Brabin, sent back rushes which Thalberg and Mayer thought so terrible they fired him. They replaced most of the cast, too—the unproven George Walsh being substituted by a studio contract artist, Ramon Novarro. Rex Ingram had hoped to direct it, but Mayer had other ideas, and a reliable company man, Fred Niblo, took over.

Here, the company shoot the sinking of the Roman trireme. Recruited locally, the extras on the ship were warned not to take the job unless they could swim—but they needed the 50 lire and took a gamble. A. Arnold Gillespie was the only representative of the company aboard. The ship caught fire when a special effect went wrong. "I thought at the time it would be a tremendous calamity," said Gillespie. "I thought we were going to lose all kinds of lives. The ship kept sinking and sinking and people were diving overboard and then coming back like bees around a piece of sugar, praying to the Madonna to save them."

Rescue boats arrived, and miraculously no lives were lost. But a few civilian clothes were left. The man in charge of wardrobe took out a rowboat and sank the clothes with chains. A couple of days later, the men came back. They had been picked up by a fishing boat and taken down the coast. Thanks to their Roman costumes, they were wined and dined as heroes. The wardrobe man apologised, and said someone must have taken their clothing by mistake . . . .

right, below] The Americans opened studios in England in the 1920s, but the films never caught on. Instead, companies made exteriors in England, and the interiors in Hollywood. Here, the Goldwyn company is at work on *Sherlock Holmes* (1922). John Barrymore as the great detective; with him is Albert S. Parker, the director, who later settled in London and ran a famous theatrical agency.

Italian workmen built Babylon for Griffith, so it was not surprising that the country of *Cabiria* could produce magnificent sets like this. *Nero* (1922) was shot in Italy by the Fox company, and directed by J. Gordon Edwards, who had made such epics as *Cleopatra* (1917) and *The Queen of Sheba* (1921). Art director John D. Braddon reconstructed ancient Rome only to burn it down at the climax. The Fox company found working in Italy difficult—extras insisted on a a siesta at noon—but director Edwards, like Henry King, admired the Italians for their friendliness and courtesy. Edwards also made a biblical picture in Jerusalem, *The Shepherd King* (1923).

below] *Madame Sans-Gêne* (1925) directed by Léonce Perret was a Paramount production starring Gloria Swanson, made on location in France—using all the locales associated with the Napoleonic period. Gloria Swanson used her influence to gain entry to the most hallowed halls of French history (this scene was shot at Fontainebleau), and the picture remains her personal favourite. Paramount might have insisted on the film being made on the backlot, but they were anxious to sign Swanson to a long-term contract, so they let her have her way.

overpage] Under the influence of documentary film maker Robert Flaherty, Hollywood made use of exotic locations for several outstandingly beautiful pictures. Flaherty was initially involved in this one— *White Shadows of the South Seas* (1928)—but quickly realised that his intuitive methods did not coincide with the more pragmatic procedures of MGM. He resigned, and W. S. Van Dyke (centre, in solar topee) took over the picture, which was shot in the South Seas. Cameraman Clyde de Vinna (second from left) won an Academy Award for his photography. Monte Blue and Raquel Torres (right of Van Dyke) were brought from Hollywood for the leading roles, but the islanders played themselves. The film depicted how the arrival of the white man had ruined the primitive communities; hence the title.

CHAPTER TWENTY

Trick of the Light

Salute to the Cameraman

The ingenuity of silent-era cameramen was astonishing. Here is
Alfred Gilks, with one of the 'nautical' Bell and Howell 2709s used
to film *Old Ironsides*. These cameras maintained their equilibrium,
no matter how great the roll of the ship. Normally, the camera
follows the pitch and toss of a ship at sea, and the horizon appears
to be tipping first one way, then another. In order to show the ship
moving, rather than the horizon, this sea-going tripod was evolved
in the Lasky camera shop, using a hydraulic method of dampening
the swing of the pendulum. The mechanical engineer responsible
was Leigh M. Griffith. The cameras were also mounted in a steel
cage, ready to be swung, along with their operators, anywhere in the
rigging. Gilks has his hand on the crank, but his camera is fitted
with a motor.

right] There can be no doubt that making silent films was a highly
enjoyable occupation. On location for a Tom Mix Western, *The
Yankee Señor* (1926); Dan Clark at camera on left, Tom Mix next to
him, Emmett Flynn, director, centre (pointing). Yellowstone
National Park.

When the Clouds Roll By was an effervescent comedy of 1919
starring Douglas Fairbanks. His former cameraman Victor Fleming
(extreme right) directed it—he later went on to make *The Wizard
of Oz* and *Gone with the Wind*. Joseph Henabery, another
Fairbanks director, helps out in this flood sequence, although
Fairbanks (pointing) seems to know just what he wants, as usual.
William McGann (right) was cameraman and Harris Thorpe
second cameraman. The picture was originally entitled *Cheer Up*;
Fairbanks's optimism caused morale to soar wherever his pictures
were shown.

right] To make a silent picture in the early days, a company
simply loaded a few vehicles and drove along dirt roads into the
countryside surrounding Los Angeles. Here a crew from the
Thomas Ince studios set up for a Douglas Maclean comedy, 1920.
Note the grip on the hood of the car on the left holding the
statutory reflector.

The location work in silent films was always one of its charms—
sound films retreated into studios when passing aircraft and the roar
of traffic made location work hazardous, slow and expensive.

Gary Cooper in a duelling scene from *Beau Sabreur* (1928) directed
by John Waters (smoking cigar, centre) for Paramount. Camera
equipment was becoming more and more sophisticated by the end
of the 'twenties, and extravagant camera movement was a distinctive
feature of the late silents. Only a major studio, however, would own
such elaborate equipment as this wheeled platform (dolly) with its
adjustable clamps for twin cameras. First cameraman C. Edgar
Schoenbaum (smoking pipe) adjusts the speed on the motor of his
Bell and Howell. A wooden guide keeps Gary Cooper within the
limits of focus. Cameras had been fitted with motors from the
beginning, but cameramen preferred to crank by hand. Motors
reappeared in the late 'twenties, although hand cranking continued
on newsreels well into the 1930s. The sight of grips, hauling the
dolly by hand, may strike a primitive note, but it's the same today.
This is clearly a posed still, otherwise the smoke from the pipe and
cigar would waft across the lens and wreck the shot.

For a dance in *Quality Street* (1927), the camera has been mounted on a swing suspended from a crane. This enables the dance to be shot in a rapid track, round and round the tree. Director Sidney Franklin at left of camera, Henrik Sartov, cameraman, in peaked cap, surveys stand-ins for the stars—Marion Davies and Conrad Nagel. Lights are also suspended from the crane, and the whole set-up has been covered with diffusing cloth. Musicians to supply the rhythm for the dance have their places below the platform.

right] Lon Chaney (left) and director Herbert Brenon at work on *Laugh Clown Laugh* (1928) with cameraman James Wong Howe. Considering the barriers of prejudice in America, such as California's Chinese exclusion laws, the success story of James Wong Howe was something of a miracle. Born in Canton, Howe came to America at the age of five. While working as a bus-boy in Beverly Hills Hotel he watched movies being shot in Chinatown and spoke to the cameraman, who suggested he tried the picture business. At the Lasky studio he was told he was too small to carry camera equipment, but he was hired to sweep up the cutting rooms. Lasky already had an Oriental cameraman—the Japanese Henry Kotani—and Howe eventually worked as his assistant. His break came when he photographed Mary Miles Minter and made her eyes dark. Miss Minter's eyes were pale blue, which registered blank on orthochromatic film. Howe had a frame of black velvet made and poked the lens through a hole in the centre. "Word got around that Mary Miles Minter had found herself a new Chinese cameraman; they thought I had been specially imported! The black velvet was something new. Soon everyone with blue eyes wanted me to photograph them, and I was launched."

below] Frank B. Good was a pioneer in the industry and an exceptionally good cameraman—although no one has ever heard of him. He was a favourite with children, and he photographed most of the Fox 'kid pictures' for the Franklin brothers. Here he poses with Jackie Coogan—both of them peering at the scene through a blue glass, which gives some idea of what it will look like in black and white.

Monsieur Beaucaire (1924), was
photographed by Harry Fischbeck,
and while surviving prints contain
none of the delicacy of the original,
this still suggests the high standard of
the lighting. The entire production was
beautifully mounted by Natacha
Rambova (Mrs Valentino), but the
direction by Sidney Olcott was far too
pedestrian to bring the story to life.
Rudolph Valentino (left) gave an
outstandingly graceful performance,
however.

643-140

CHAPTER TWENTY ONE

More than Meets the Eye

Salute to the Art Director

The craft of the cameraman and the art director were closely interlinked, for one could not operate without the other. In the realm of special effects—such as this hanging miniature of a castle, which is not built full size on that hill, but merely suspended at the end of the set—the registration had to be precise. A production shot from *Monte Cristo* (1922), directed by Emmett Flynn and photographed by Lucien Andriot. Art director William Darling.

Art direction in films followed as a logical progression from stage
design. The realism and the striking lighting effects of Belasco were
reflected in the work of DeMille and Griffith, while Maurice
Tourneur and his art director Ben Carré experimented by
returning to first essentials with the story-book simplicity of
Prunella (1918). Both Tourneur and Carré had served their
apprenticeship in the French theatre; the importance of their
contribution to the American cinema has only recently been
acknowledged. (Jules Raucourt and Marguerite Clark.)

left] Part of the sets of old Paris erected at Griffith Mamaroneck, N.Y. studio for *Orphans of the Storm* by art director Charles M. Kirk. Always invigorated by competition, this film was Griffith's reply to such German historical pictures as *Madame Dubarry*— which reconstructed the French revolution on a grand scale. The German films were aided by rampant unemployment, which made extras both plentiful and cheap. Griffith made sure his film was even more spectacular, but his concentration on big pictures tied up his studio and made it unprofitable. In this scene, Lillian Gish realises that the girl begging in the street is her sister—see page 62.

Universal was the silent era's sausage factory, churning out series after series, programme picture after programme picture. Lacking theatre chains in the big cities, it aimed its subject matter at small town and rural audiences, who were considered to be less demanding. Once in a while, however, a massive prestige picture was put into production; perhaps the most famous was *The Phantom of the Opera* (1925). One of the art directors was Ben Carré, familiar with the Paris Opera House from his days as a stage designer in France. He was entrusted with all the scenes in the catacombs, from which this is a striking example. (The cameraman was Charles van Enger.) Carré had worked for years with Maurice Tourneur, and must share the credit for his achievements. After a brilliant career as art director, Carré, in the 1930s, returned to his first love, the painting of massive backdrops—and continued at MGM until the 1960s.

right] The art direction in German pictures was often superb, and the envy of Hollywood. This scene is from Ernst Lubitsch's *Loves of Pharaoh* (1922) with sets by Erno Metzner, Ernst Stern and Kurt Richter. Architectural consultant, Max Gronau. Lubitsch brought this picture over to America, and attended the première of Griffith's *Orphans of the Storm*, which owed something to his own *Madame Dubarry*.

In most American pictures, a streetcorner was photographed as a streetcorner. But the Germans had a totally different attitude to film design. When F. W. Murnau was brought over by William Fox to make *Sunrise* (1927), he was given a free hand. Murnau's designer, Rochus Gliese, constructed a city at the Fox studios. The film was an artistic triumph, but Fox was appalled at the size of the budget.

Having been impressed by the construction camp scenes in Frank
Borzage's *The River* (1928), I asked the cameraman, Ernest Palmer,
where they had been shot—Northern California? Oregon? "On the
backlot," he replied. It is a tribute to Harry Oliver's art direction
that I still find it hard to believe.

Ernest Palmer is second from right in this line-up, with the star,
Charles Farrell third from right; Frank Borzage at extreme left,
Harry Oliver at extreme left.

Programme Credits

Written, directed and produced by David Gill and Kevin Brownlow

Executive producer Mike Wooller   *Narrator* James Mason

Ted Adcock *Cameraman*
David Bradley *Adviser*
Eric Brazier *Sound recordist*
Dan Carter *Film editor*
Carl Davis *Music*
Bob Dyer *Assistant editor*
William K. Everson *Adviser*
Raye Farr *Associate producer/Film research*
Jacqui French *Additional stills research*
Anne Gibbs *Production assistant*
Jenny Holt *Assembly editor*
Leslie Hope–Stern *Graphics*
Jeremy Isaacs *Special consultant*
John Kobal *Stills consultant*

Bessie Love *Historical adviser*
Mike Maddison *Film research*
Sue McConachy *Associate producer*
Barry O'Riordan *Graphics*
Hari Ryatt *Assistant editor*
Richard Schickel *American consultant*
David Shepard *Adviser*
Freddie Slade *Dubbing mixer*
Liz Sutherland *Production manager*
Ron Thomas *Sound recordist*
Trevor Waite *Supervising film editor*
Oscar Webb *Film editor*
Pam Willis *Production assistant*
John Wright *Assistant editor*

Still Photographers' Credits

Abbe 177, 180, 238/239
Gene Aestep 104/105
Albin 224
Apeda-New York 265
Fred Archer 21
Ernest Bachrach 132, 133, 252/253
Milton Browne 195
C. S. Bull 129
Wallace Chewning 131, 237, 260, 263
Robert Coburn 173
Frank Diem 242
Otto Dyar 12, 24, 234, 258, 259
Don English 179
Nelson Evans 96 (bottom), 97 (bottom), 98/99, 147 (top), 168, 176, 200
Jack Freulich 22/23, 138, 139, 255, 256, 257
Elmer Fryer 207
William Grimes 16, 124, 127, 198, 199, 201 (both), 213
Hartsook 106, 107, 162
Fred Hendrickson 19

George Hommel 217
Ray Jones 219
Donald Biddle Keyes 89 (top), 117, 122/123, 169, 190, 191
Gene Kornman 140, 141, 154/155
Madison Lacy 126, 254
Bud Longworth 182/183, 243
Ruth Harriet Louise 125
James Manatt 20, 210, 212, 266
Arthur Marion 128, 235
John Miehle 244
Fred Morgan 175
Frank Powolny 25, 167, 231, 246, 262
K. O. Rahm 165
Rice 15, 148/149, 187, 188, 189, 215
E. R. Richee 130, 178
Charles Rosher 163
Karl Struss 170
C. Warrength 164
Witzel 160, 161

Culver Pictures 32, 42, 43, 45, 50, 51, 52, 84, 87, 137, 165
Marc Wanamaker/Bison Archives 67 (bottom), 76, 83, 94, 97 (top), 115
Bob Birchard 93, 120
Arnold Cillespie 225 (top)

John Kobal would like to thank the following for those stills which do not come from his own collection:

Kevin Brownlow 12, 13, 14, 18, 20, 25, 57, 59, 60, 66, 69, 100, 102, 103, 114, 116, 117, 132, 133, 138, 139, 146, 151, 159, 163, 171, 172, 173, 174, 186, 188, 190, 194, 198, 206, 207, 214, 215, 217, 218, 219, 220/221, 222, 223 (top and bottom), 225 (bottom), 226, 230, 231, 232, 234, 236, 238/239, 240, 243, 246, 247, 251, 256, (top), 261, 262

He would also like to thank the following individuals for their help in the preparation of this book: Carlos Clarens, Hilary Downie, Howard Mandelbaum and Frank Powolny.

Interviewed for the Television Series

Stars and other players
Mary Astor
Eleanor Boardman
Louise Brooks
Olive Carey (*wife of Harry Carey*)
Jackie Coogan
Dolores Costello (*wife of John Barrymore*)
Viola Dana
Douglas Fairbanks Jr
Janet Gaynor
Lillian Gish
Neil Hamilton
George Harris (*English comedian taken to Hollywood by Sennett*)
Al Hoxie
Leatrice Joy (*wife of John Gilbert*)
Bessie Love
Ben Lyon
Marion Mack
Percy Marmont
Col. Tim McCoy
Colleen Moore
Charles 'Buddy' Rogers
Benny Rubin (*Vaudeville comedian*)
Eva von Berne
Valerie von Stroheim (*dress extra and wife of Erich*)
Gloria Swanson
Blanche Sweet
John Wayne (*property man at the time*)
Lois Wilson

Directors
Dorothy Arzner (*editor, later director*)
Clarence Brown
Frank Capra (*gag man for Sennett, later director*)
George Cukor (*dialogue director, later director*)
Allan Dwan
Henry Hathaway (*property man, later director*)
Howard Hawks (*also writer and producer*)
Henry King
Mervyn LeRoy (*gag man, later director*)
Lewis Milestone
Al Rogell
King Vidor
William Wyler (*assistant, later director*)

Producers
Irving Asher
Paul Kohner
Hal Roach

Cameramen
Lucien Andriot
Karl Brown (*Bitzer's assistant, then cameraman and later director*)
George Folsey
Lee Garmes
Byron Haskin
Paul Ivano

Art director
A. Arnold Gillespie

Property man
R. Lee 'Lefty' Hough (*later Fox studio manager*)

Editors
William Hornbeck (*with Mack Sennett*)
Harold Schuster (*actor, then editor and later director*)
Grant Whytock (*with Rex Ingram*)

Stunt men and women
Yakima Canutt
Mrs Buck Jones (*stunt rider and wife of Buck Jones*)
Paul Malvern
Harvey Parry
Bob Rose
Iron Eyes Cody (*Indian actor and technical adviser*)

Musicians
Gaylord Carter
Chauncey Haines

Writers
Cedric Belfrage
Anita Loos
Sam Marx (*story editor at MGM*)
Adela Rogers St Johns

Relatives and others
Leatrice Gilbert Fountain (*daughter of Leatrice Joy and John Gilbert*)
Agnes de Mille (*daughter of William, niece of Cecil*)
Alberto Valentino (*brother of Rudolph*)
Jean Valentino (*nephew of Rudolph*)
Jessy Lasky Jr (*son of producer Jesse L. Lasky*)
Lord Mountbatten (*a guest at "Pickfair"*)
Mary Paige (*a fan*)

rear endpaper] After dickering with the idea of sound, accepting the idea, then rejecting it, Metro-Goldwyn-Mayer finally make the symbolic gesture—and record Leo, the lion, for the trademark. December 18, 1928. The silent era is over.